SEP 2 1981

THE GREEK TRAGEDY
IN NEW TRANSLATIONS

GENERAL EDITOR William Arrowsmith

EURIPIDES: The Phoenician Women

EURIPIDES

The Phoenician Women

Translated by
PETER BURIAN
and
BRIAN SWANN

New York   Oxford
OXFORD UNIVERSITY PRESS
1981

Library of Congress Cataloging in Publication Data

Euripides.
The Phoenician women.

(Greek tragedy in new translations)
I. Burian, Peter.   II. Swann, Brian.
III. Title.   IV. Series.
PA3975.P6 1981   882'.01   81-5085
ISBN 0-19-502923-2   AACR2

Printing (last digit): 987654321

Printed in the United States of America

EDITOR'S FOREWORD

The Greek Tragedy in New Translations is based on the conviction
that poets like Aeschylus, Sophocles, and Euripides can only be
properly rendered by translators who are themselves poets. Scholars
may, it is true, produce useful and perceptive versions. But our most
urgent present need is for a *re-creation* of these plays—as though they
had been written, freshly and greatly, by masters fully at home in the
English of our own times. Unless the translator is a poet, his original
is likely to reach us in crippled form: deprived of the power and perti-
nence it must have if it is to speak to us of what is permanent in the
Greek. But poetry is not enough; the translator must obviously know
what he is doing, or he is bound to do it badly. Clearly, few contemporary poets possess enough Greek to undertake the complex and
formidable task of transplanting a Greek play without also "colonial-
izing" it or stripping it of its deep cultural difference, its remoteness
from us. And that means depriving the play of that crucial *otherness*
of Greek experience—a quality no less valuable to us than its close-
ness. Collaboration between scholar and poet is therefore the essential operating principle of the series. In fortunate cases scholar and
poet co-exist; elsewhere we have teamed able poets and scholars in an
effort to supply, through affinity and intimate collaboration, the necessary combination of skills.

An effort has been made to provide the general reader or student
with first-rate critical introductions, clear expositions of translators'
principles, commentary on difficult passages, ample stage directions,
and glossaries of mythical and geographical terms encountered in the
plays. Our purpose throughout has been to make the reading of the

plays as vivid as possible. But our poets have constantly tried to remember that they were translating *plays*—plays meant to be produced, in language that actors could speak, naturally and with dignity. The poetry aims at being *dramatic* poetry and realizing itself in words and actions that are both speakable and playable.

Finally, the reader should perhaps be aware that no pains have been spared in order that the "minor" plays should be translated as carefully and brilliantly as the acknowledged masterpieces. For the Greek Tragedy in New Translations aims to be, in the fullest sense, *new*. If we need vigorous new poetic versions, we also need to see the plays with fresh eyes, to reassess the plays for ourselves, in terms of our own needs. This means translations that liberate us from the canons of an earlier age because the translators have recognized, and discovered, in often neglected works, the perceptions and wisdom that make these works ours and necessary to us.

A NOTE ON THE SERIES FORMAT

If only for the illusion of coherence, a series of thirty-three Greek plays requires a consistent format. Different translators, each with his individual voice, cannot possibly develop the sense of a single coherent style for each of the three tragedians; nor even the illusion that, despite their differences, the tragedians share a common set of conventions and a generic, or period, style. But they can at least share a common approach to orthography and a common vocabulary of conventions.

1. *Spelling of Greek names*
Adherence to the old convention whereby Greek names were first Latinized before being housed in English is gradually disappearing. We are now clearly moving away from Latinization and toward precise transliteration. The break with tradition may be regrettable, but there is much to be said for hearing and seeing Greek names as though they were both Greek and new, instead of Roman or neoclassical importations. We cannot of course see them as wholly new. For better or worse certain names and myths are too deeply rooted in our literature and thought to be dislodged. To speak of "Helene" and "Hekabe" would be no less pedantic and absurd than to write "Aischylos" or "Platon" or "Thoukydides." There are of course borderline cases. "Jocasta" (as opposed to "Iokaste") is not a major mythical figure in her own right; her familiarity in her Latin form is a function of the fame of Sophocles' play as the tragedy *par excel-*

lence. And as tourists we go to Delphi, not Delphoi. The precisely transliterated form may be pedantically "right," but the pedantry goes against the grain of cultural habit and actual usage.

As a general rule, we have therefore adopted a "mixed" orthography according to the principles suggested above. When a name has been firmly housed in English (admittedly the question of domestication is often moot), the traditional spelling has been kept. Otherwise names have been transliterated. Throughout the series the -os termination of masculine names has been adopted, and Greek diphthongs (as in Iphigenia) have normally been retained. We cannot expect complete agreement from readers (or from translators, for that matter) about borderline cases. But we want at least to make the operative principle clear: to walk a narrow line between orthographical extremes in the hope of keeping what should not, if possible, be lost; and refreshing, in however tenuous a way, the specific sound and name-boundedness of Greek experience.

2. Stage directions

The ancient manuscripts of the Greek plays do not supply stage directions (though the ancient commentators often provide information relevant to staging, delivery, "blocking," etc.). Hence stage directions must be inferred from words and situations and our knowledge of Greek theatrical conventions. At best this is a ticklish and uncertain procedure. But it is surely preferable that good stage directions should be provided by the translator than that the reader should be left to his own devices in visualizing action, gesture, and spectacle. Obviously the directions supplied should be both spare and defensible. Ancient tragedy was austere and "distanced" by means of masks, which means that the reader must not expect the detailed intimacy ("He shrugs and turns wearily away," "She speaks with deliberate slowness, as though to emphasize the point," etc.) which characterizes stage directions in modern naturalistic drama. Because Greek drama is highly rhetorical and stylized, the translator knows that his words must do the real work of inflection and nuance. Therefore every effort has been made to supply the visual and tonal sense required by a given scene and the reader's (or actor's) putative unfamiliarity with the ancient conventions.

3. Numbering of lines

For the convenience of the reader who may wish to check the English against the Greek text or vice versa, the lines have been numbered according to both the Greek text and the translation. The lines of the English translation have been numbered in multiples of ten, and these numbers have been set in the right-hand margin. The (inclusive) Greek numeration will be found bracketed at the top of the page. The reader will doubtless note that in many plays the English lines outnumber the Greek, but he should not therefore conclude that the translator has been unduly prolix. In most cases the reason is simply that the translator has adopted the free-flowing norms of modern Anglo-American prosody, with its brief, breath- and emphasis-determined lines, and its habit of indicating cadence and caesuras by line length and setting rather than by conventional punctuation. Other translators have preferred four-beat or five-beat lines, and in these cases Greek and English numerations will tend to converge.

4. *Notes and Glossary*

In addition to the Introduction, each play has been supplemented by Notes (identified by the line numbers of the translation) and a Glossary. The Notes are meant to supply information which the translators deem important to the interpretation of a passage; they also afford the translator an opportunity to justify what he has done. The Glossary is intended to spare the reader the trouble of going elsewhere to look up mythical or geographical terms. The entries are not meant to be comprehensive; when a fuller explanation is needed, it will be found in the Notes.

ON THE TRANSLATORS

Brian Swann, educated at Cambridge and Princeton, is at present Associate Professor of English at The Cooper Union in New York City. An exceptionally versatile and prolific writer, his publications include contributions of poetry, fiction, criticism, and translation to more than two hundred journals. He is the author of four volumes of poetry, two collections of short stories, a novella, and a novel, as well as numerous translations from Italian (the poetry of Lucio Piccolo, Zanzotto, Scotellaro, Cattafi, Levi, and Bodini) in collaboration with Ruth Feldman; collaborative translations from Turkish (Anday); and versions of Arghezi's and Tzara's work from Rumanian. In addition, he has edited a volume entitled *Smoothing the Ground: Essays on Native American Oral Literature* (for the American Indian Studies Center of the University of California), and will soon publish a volume of versions of American Indian poetry.

Swann's collaborator, Peter Burian, is presently Associate Professor of Classical Studies at Duke University. In 1972–73 he was awarded a fellowship for research on Euripides by the National Endowment for the Humanities; in 1981 he was appointed a fellow of the Center for Hellenic Studies in Washington. A translator of Italian and classical poetry, he is also the author of several penetrating critical articles on Sophocles' *Oedipus at Kolonos* and Euripides' *The Children of Herakles*. His current research project is a full-scale study of Euripidean drama.

ON THE TRANSLATION

One of the operating premises of the Oxford series is that good translation requires not only first-rate scholarly mediation, both specific and general, but the application of fine critical intelligence. It was at any rate our hope that the series might provide the Greekless reader with the discursive critical reading that had informed the translation but that could also confirm and amplify it in another dimension. Professor Burian is that *rara avis* in classical studies (a profession which has always felt uneasy with literary criticism as opposed to philological skills), a fine scholar endowed with unusual critical judgment and persuasiveness. And his reading of *The Phoenician Women*, especially in this discussion of the play's structure and symbolism—the fatal ambivalence of man as unstable compound of beast and god, baseness and nobility—is not only convincing in itself but marks, I believe, a real advance in our general understanding of Euripides and also of this unjustly neglected and strangely compelling—though admittedly very odd, very Euripidean—play.

Armed with Burian's sensitive reading, Swann for his part takes the risks required by the play's structural reversals and deliberate incongruities of tone and texture. The swift, almost breathless pace of the original, represented metrically by the translator's basically five-beat loping lines and constant run-ons, sustains the original's headlong rushing of events, scene after scene of contrasting tableaux and themes almost cinematic in their rapidity of tempo and metaphorical vividness. Swann's rhetoric and diction are spare; sparer, I suppose, than Euripides'. But intentionally so. There is simply no modern metrical or rhetorical convention capable of coping with the dramatist's mercurial shifts of tone, from elevated to colloquial, from tragic to pathetic, noble to base. If he is honest, if he cares more for his original than for the figure he might cut by making Euripides the vehicle of his own ambitions or poetics, the translator will rigorously refrain from smoothing out the jagged surface and often jarringly abrupt transitions of the original. This is what Swann has done. The result is what the translators call an "enactment," a true dramatic script of a play meant to be sung and danced. Here, if you like, is an amplified poetic libretto. Conscientiously—that is, honestly and directly, with unassuming candor and freshness—the translators commend their version of the original to the reader's critical intelligence and theatrical imagination, and, not unreasonably, to the animating hope of sympathetic performance.

Baltimore and New York   William Arrowsmith

CONTENTS

Introduction, 3

The Phoenician Women, 19

Notes, 87

Glossary, 97

THE PHOENICIAN WOMEN

INTRODUCTION

I

Euripides' *Phoenician Women*, esteemed in antiquity, is largely despised or neglected today. And in truth, it is not an easy play to understand, or to like. Many have despaired of finding coherence in its profusion, in so much seemingly frigid pathos with no clear emotional center, so many characters with no hero, such a welter of events with no obvious organizing principle. Some have called it a pageant rather than a drama, as if that distinction obviated the need for cohesion. Others have seen it as thinly disguised political allegory, claiming apparent faults of construction as proof of some hidden intent. Still others have performed more or less radical philological surgery on the received text, in hopes of saving the evidently good limbs and organs. Finally, a few have sought out themes and images that bind the various episodes more or less closely together, but generally stopped short of demonstrating the coherence of the drama as a whole.[1]

To begin with, let us recognize that what the author of the third

1. Literary (as opposed to strictly philological) studies of the *Phoenician Women* are not numerous. We have found the following recent work of value: A. J. Podlecki, "Some themes in Euripides' *Phoenissae*," *Transactions of the American Philological Association* 93 (1962), 355-73; D. J. Conacher, *Euripidean Drama* (London and Toronto, 1967), 227-48; J. de Romilly, "*Phoenician Women* of Euripides: Topicality in Greek Tragedy," *Bucknell Review* 15 (1967), 108-32; E. Rawson, "Family and Fatherland in Euripides' *Phoenissae*," *Greek, Roman, and Byzantine Studies* 11 (1970), 109-27. We owe a special debt of gratitude to a new and enlightening study by Marilyn B. Arthur, "The Curse of Civilization: The Choral Odes of the *Phoenissae*," *Harvard Studies in Classical Philology* 81 (1977), 163-85.

3

argument found in our manuscripts already singled out for criticism, "overfull and episodic construction," is a deliberate and crucial part of Euripides' dramatic strategy. Far from concentrating on a single issue, Euripides is at pains to include as much as he can fit in. He allows Jokasta to survive to see her sons' death before killing herself, and then brings Oedipus on to mourn them all. Apparently unwilling to choose between the two ends that the tradition awarded Antigone, he takes them both (if our text of the *exodos* is so far to be trusted) and, over the protest of an outraged scholiast, sends Antigone off to brave Kreon's wrath by burying Polyneikes, and to accompany her blind old father into exile. The Phoenician maidens of the Chorus, caught at Thebes by the outbreak of war while on their way to Delphi, depict themselves as distant relatives of Kadmos, the Phoenician who founded Thebes, and then go on to rehearse Theban history from the very beginning. And lest we regard this as mere poetic window-dressing, Euripides makes Kreon's son Menoikeus sacrifice himself, at the bidding of the seer Teiresias, by leaping into the cave of the dragon that Kadmos had killed long ago, in order to placate Ares' lingering anger at its slaying and thus to save the city.

This sheer luxuriance of material is what everyone notices right away about the *Phoenician Women*, but its formal organization tends to be overlooked. The material is not, as is often alleged, loosely strung together; on the contrary, it is shaped into a structure of almost alarming rigor.[2] The central episode is—of all things—Menoikeus' sacrifice. Around it the other scenes are ranged in axial symmetry. Jokasta's prologue, setting out the troubled history of Laios' house, is answered at the end of the drama by the survivors, Oedipus, Antigone, and Kreon, considering its bleak future. Similarly, Antigone's lyric contemplation of the Argive army drawn up for battle in the *teichoskopia* that follows Jokasta's monologue is answered after the battle by her lyric monody of lament, which then becomes a duet with Oedipus. And the long episode in which Jokasta fails to reconcile Eteokles and Polyneikes is brought to fulfillment at the beginning of the *exodos* in the messenger's description of the duel that proved fatal to both sons and their mother. Around the central episode itself are the scene in which Kreon and Eteokles plan for the coming battle, and the messenger's report of the Theban victory in that battle. Furthermore, as we shall see, the choral lyrics that frame these episodes are a close-knit song cycle evoking the legendary and miraculous past in whose context the action of the drama takes on its full meaning.

2. Cf. W. Ludwig, "Sapheneia" (diss., Tübingen, 1955), esp. 130-35.

II

So far then, we have described a welter of matter in an intricate formal framework. If we can relate the two, we shall perhaps have a cogent account of the play's peculiarities and the beginnings of an interpretation. We have seen that the sacrifice of Menoikeus is the formal epicenter. Given that the play's primary concern is with the fate of the house of Laios, represented by no fewer than five of its most famous figures, is it not odd that Euripides should give pride of place to an otherwise practically unattested son of Kreon, whose noble act he may well have invented for the occasion?[3] And that Menoikeus' function should be to redeem the land of Thebes not from Oedipus' pollution or the curse that rests on his sons, but from Ares' wrath at the slaying of a serpent so long ago? It is evident that Euripides is playing with the received mythical tradition. One is reminded of the free invention that characterized the roughly contemporary Orestes. Does the tradition (embodied, for example, in Aeschylus' Seven Against Thebes and Sophocles' Antigone) treat Eteokles as the high-minded defender of his city's freedom against a foreign foe? Euripides makes naked ambition for power the ruling passion of this Eteokles to the exclusion of any love for his country or his family. "Let the whole house fall to ruin!" Eteokles tells his mother, and in what were apparently the play's most famous lines in antiquity (often quoted, we are told, by Julius Caesar) he expresses a philosophy worthy of Plato's Thrasymachos: "This one thing makes wrong right: power." Is Polyneikes, the "man of much strife" as his name suggests, traditionally the very figure of rebellious daring? Euripides gives this Polyneikes a timid entrance, skittish at every noise and every movement despite the truce his mother has arranged, and brings out in him strains of concern for his family and affection for his native place that seem almost to belie the fact that he is leading an Argive army to sack the city. Is Kreon the advocate par excellence of the claims of the state over those of the family? When Teiresias informs this Kreon that his son must die to save the state, he replies without a moment's hesitation (1057-58),* "I wasn't listening. I didn't hear. / City, goodbye!" and goes on to plot Menoikeus' escape.

And so it goes. But this play with tradition is by no means an isolated phenomenon, an end in itself. Euripides is never concerned

---

3. F. Vian, Les Origines de Thèbes (Paris, 1963), 206-15, marshals evidence for previous versions of this episode, but the results are inconclusive.

* Unless otherwise indicated, line references throughout are to the English version.

simply to criticize his predecessors or "correct" their telling of the old tales. His innovations—even where, as in much of his later work, they court a self-conscious and rather brittle literariness—always serve a larger purpose. In the case of the *Phoenician Women*, Euripides' peculiar treatment of both plot and character emphasizes elements of volition and choice. The story of course brings with it all the trappings of fatality—curse, prophecy, foreboding—and yet everything that happens is grounded most circumstantially in the workings of the will.

The point can perhaps best be made by examining the great debate of the brothers whom Jokasta has brought together in hopes of a reconciliation. Here, Euripides seems almost to abandon the world of myth in favor of a version of contemporary reality. All three speakers couch their arguments in elaborate and self-conscious specimens of the new sophistic rhetoric, full of neat antitheses, clever paradoxes, and aphoristic climaxes. Eteokles justifies his unrelenting ambition with the will-to-power ethics of the unabashed tyrant,[4] and Jokasta answers with an Athenian democrat's praise of equality as the foundation of civilized life. Polyneikes dwells on the hardships of exile, a very real element of contemporary experience and an important theme in this play. But by pressing his rightful claim on what is his—a share in the rule of Thebes—Polyneikes becomes a traitor to the city he has come to sack, if he cannot win it by negotiation. And of course he cannot. The point of this elaborate debate, as of many others in Euripides, is precisely its inability to change the course of an action already fixed by the passionate intransigence of the agents. Eteokles' whole bag of rhetorical tricks and philosophical conundrums is not really designed to persuade his interlocutors; he is simply restating his refusal to yield what he wants—and already has—merely because someone else wants it, too. Polyneikes makes it clear that he will press his claim no matter what the cost. Jokasta neatly beats both brothers at their own rhetorical game, but her refutation of one's ambition and the other's treason does not budge either a bit. Eteokles caps her speech by declaring that (639) "the war is words no more," and in the acrimonious stichomythy that closes the *episode* both brothers merely illustrate once more the disastrous failings of which she has convicted them.[5]

4. W. R. Connor, "Tyrannos Polis," *Ancient and Modern: Essays in Honor of Gerald F. Else* (Ann Arbor, 1977), 95-109, makes the useful point that eagerness to acquire tyranny is rooted in commonly accepted Greek attitudes. We cannot assume that an Athenian would regard Eteokles as simply idiosyncratic or depraved.

5. This point is neatly emphasized in the messenger's account of the fatal duel,

The debate scene embodies the central change that Euripides has made in the legendary material, and has indeed elevated to one of the organizing principles of his play. This we might call the triumph of self-interest, with its concomitant reduction to chaos and arbitrariness of the whole nexus of relations within family and community. To put it baldly, Euripides takes the story of a fated fall and transforms it into a story of self-destruction through the passionate pursuit of selfish ends. We must immediately add that this is only one part of a complex dialectic; we shall shortly see fatality at work in a somewhat unexpected form. And yet, over against the legendary tradition, there can be no doubt of the force of Euripides' innovation. To take the most obvious example, the conscious choice of each brother to kill the other in order to rule alone makes of their mutual slaughter something willful and even gratuitous in a way that it is not in Aeschylus' *Seven Against Thebes*. This is underlined in the episode that follows the debate, in which Eteokles plans battle strategy with Kreon. In Aeschylus, Eteokles' considered choice of warriors to face the Argive captains finally and horribly leaves only himself to defend the seventh gate against his brother, and thus, as he recognizes, to fulfill Oedipus' curse. In Euripides, Kreon, after considering several ill-advised suggestions of Eteokles, proposes selecting seven captains to stand at the gates. Eteokles agrees, with the remark that it would be too time-consuming to name their names, but that he hopes to have his brother set against him, and to kill him. This is surely not, as is often supposed, a cheap shot at Aeschylus, but rather a clear statement of Euripides' vastly different purpose: to show his characters actively pursuing destructive and self-destructive ends, not being reluctantly overtaken by their fates. The Euripidean Eteokles, like the Aeschylean, is aware of his father's curse, and indeed refers to it just after announcing his desire to meet his brother in battle. But the reference is framed as a curiously detached, almost sardonic reproach against Oedipus (869-72):

> When my father put out
> his eyes, he proved himself a fool. I cannot
> praise him, for he knew that his curses
> might kill us.

---

where Jokasta's sarcastic reproaches of her sons are unwittingly echoed by their friends as encouragement. Compare, for example, "Polyneikes, you can set up a statue to Zeus as trophy, and give glory to Argos" with Jokasta's sarcastic "What trophies can you dedicate to Zeus?"

Eteokles' recognition of his father's curse is clearly no more a deterrent to him in the pursuit of his ambition than the arguments of justice and fair play.

Euripides, rehearsing in 410 B.C. (the likely date of composition of the *Phoenician Women*) the old tale of the fall of the house of Laios, could hardly have missed the chance it afforded to dramatize the factional strife, the ruthless jockeying for power, the easy equation of personal advantage with common good, that were to prove so ruinous for Athens. This was the season of Alkibiades' return from exile, and it is interesting to see that words which Thucydides puts into the mouth of the brilliant Athenian renegade in a speech to the Spartans could, if recast in verse, almost be spoken by the Polyneikes of our play:

> I have no love for my city when it does me wrong, but only when it gives me my rights. Indeed, I do not consider myself to be attacking my own country, but rather to be rewinning a country that is mine no longer. The man who really loves his city, if he loses it unjustly, will not refrain from attack; on the contrary, desire will lead him to try anything to get it back.
>
> [*The Peloponnesian War*, VI, 92.4]

This is not to say that the *Phoenician Women* is about Alkibiades, or the struggle of Athenian factions, or that it is designed to further the policy of reconciliation of exiles, or to oppose it. Rather, Euripides seems to feel (as does Thucydides) that at the root of the political crisis in Athens is the loosing of civic ties, the replacement of public interest with the conflicting, largely selfish interests of individuals and groups within the state. The themes of self-seeking and self-destruction in the *Phoenician Women* are the dramatic expression of this civic concern.

III

Self-destruction is opposed by self-sacrifice, self-seeking by selfless dedication to the common good in the Menoikeus episode. The contrast of Menoikeus' attitude with that of his cousins in the debate scene, and of his own father here, could hardly be more striking. To the revelation by Teiresias of Ares' strange and sudden demand that a pure victim descended from the sown-men be sacrificed to avenge the dragon once slain by Kadmos, Kreon reacts as we might expect Polyneikes or Eteokles to in the same circumstances (1103-04): "I'll never sink so low that I'd / slaughter my son to ransom my city." Kreon's privatism where his own personal concerns are at stake is such that he does not stop to weigh alternatives or debate the issue with himself. The conclusion is foregone, and Kreon moves headlong into the task of getting his son out of town before anyone else finds out about Teiresias' oracle. But for Menoikeus the opposite conclusion is equally foregone. He shrewdly does not try to argue with his father; instead he tricks him into leaving by artful dissimulation, and then announces his true intention. Rather than earn the reproach of cowardice and betray family and fatherland by going into exile, he will offer his soul to save the city and free his native soil.

Menoikeus is one of a line of noble young idealists in Euripidean drama who give their lives for what they see as a higher purpose.[6] Each case is different and must be interpreted in its own dramatic context, but all share certain characteristics, including an essential isolation of the victims from the world that surrounds them. The victims' youth is not only a function of whatever ritual or narrative reason is adduced in the text, it is a token of an innocence essential to the meaning of their deeds. Makaria, in the early *Children of Herakles*, offers her life spontaneously and without reservation so that her brothers and sisters will not have to leave the refuge they have found at last in Attica from the ruthless King Eurystheus. She appears and disappears even more abruptly than Menoikeus, an emblem of nobility and self-sacrifice, unsullied by any ambition beyond winning glory for her deed, freely choosing honor over life itself. Iphigeneia in the *Iphigeneia at Aulis*, perhaps Euripides' last play, is a much more fully developed, and much more equivocal, figure than Makaria, but when she realizes the inevitability of her slaughter, she turns it into self-sacrifice by the same impulses toward generosity and glory that prompted Makaria. We are free to regard her belief that she is dying for Greek freedom as self-delusion; it is nevertheless impossible to overlook the love for her father (whose weakness she alone in the play does not recognize), the desire to prove herself worthy of her noble line, and the longing for lasting honor that propel her to the sacrificial altar. As Aristotle says of the young, they prefer the noble to the convenient, following their natural bent rather than calculation. (*Rhetoric* II, 12.)

---

6. Other figures of self-sacrifice in Euripides are Alcestis in the play that bears her name, and Evadne in the *Suppliant Women*, although the latter's self-immolation on her husband's pyre is demanded by no one, serves no communal function, and indeed seems almost a parody of the heroism of the other Euripidean victims.

Menoikeus is such a youthful idealist in a play otherwise dominated by the willful and the self-seeking. (Jokasta of course is neither, but she is also totally ineffectual.) His self-sacrifice offers a distinctive, but isolated, image of civic responsibility and the relationship of the individual to family and community. Euripides has chosen to place at the center of his play a vision of self-sacrificing patriotism that emphatically deflects the main story line, but lights up a stage upon which the city has until now been only the object of conflicting claims and ambitions. The illumination is only momentary, however, for after Menoikeus' departure we return to the same kind of "realism" (as everyone calls it for lack of a better word) which we observed in the first half of the play. The sacrifice itself appears again only as a pathetic incident (chiefly in Kreon's laments); its effect on the city's survival is given only the most casual mention, as at the beginning of the brilliant messenger speech that describes Thebes' victory. The single combat by which Eteokles and Polyneikes agree to settle their conflict, and the fate of Thebes, embodies in an active and decisive form the desire of each to kill the other simply to achieve his own ends. Antigone's lyric dirge turns the focus of the drama definitively toward the private and pathetic. Oedipus emerges from his solitude to mourn the sons whom his curse has killed and the wife who has chosen to join them in death, but above all to lament his own miserable fate.

When Kreon tells Oedipus that the city's well-being demands his expulsion, he answers purely in terms of personal pathos (1788-89): "Why are you killing me, Kreon? For you / do kill me if you cast me out of this land." This equation of exile with death (Polyneikes, thinking of the exile's lack of political freedom, had merely called it slavery) neatly reverses Menoikeus' choice of death for the city's well-being over shameful exile. Antigone casts her lot with Oedipus and chooses exile over marriage to Haimon, a choice sometimes said to be like that of Menoikeus in its self-sacrifice. But Antigone, like Oedipus, regards exile only as a matter of personal suffering, not of her country's best interest. And her passionate rejection of Kreon's attempt to insist on the marriage (she threatens to become another Danaid and slay her bridegroom, and Kreon the family man immediately relents) has more of the self-willed ruthlessness of Oedipus' sons than the selflessness of Kreon's. As regards Kreon's political wisdom, since it includes not only the exile of Oedipus but the denial of burial to Polyneikes enjoined on him by Eteokles, we cannot help viewing it with a certain suspicion.

At the center of the *Phoehician Women*, then, is one deliberately isolated scene of ideal civic heroism, issuing in the play's only act grounded in a true understanding of the relation of self to family and state. Yet it is an act of self-destruction, and one moreover whose meaning the rest of the drama manages successfully to ignore. By reversing the play's leading terms of self-interest, the Menoikeus episode embodies a standard which can be held up to the action as a whole. The structure that results is not particularly comfortable, but it is by no means incoherent, either. It contains the direct expression of its own limitation, the self-examination of a vision deeply felt and profoundly disturbing.

IV

The Menoikeus episode is central to the *Phoenician Women* in another way, as well, for it links the dramatic action directly to the early history of Thebes, which until this point has been largely restricted to the choral lyrics. Now it becomes clear that Theban saga, far from performing a purely decorative function, must be understood as a determinant of the events we are witnessing. Teiresias announces that, for Thebes to be victorious, Ares requires a descendant of the men sprung from serpent's teeth to sacrifice his life in repayment for Kadmos' killing of the serpent. Menoikeus responds to the demand with a fatal leap into the monster's very lair. Why this curiously archaizing and exotic turn of events in a play so heavily infused with an atmosphere of fifth-century *realpolitik*?

We can start to answer the question by observing that Euripides has been careful from the outset to establish links between Thebes' past and the play's present. Jokasta opens her prologue by lamenting the day that Kadmos came to Thebes, thus connecting her present sorrows with the city's very foundation. But it is the Chorus that systematically unfold the tale of Thebes' past, preparing us for the moment when it merges with the present. The Chorus are Phoenicians, like Kadmos, and they have repeated his journey. They are moreover related to the Thebans through common descent from Io. Thus, while foreigners not directly affected by the action, they can be expected to show more than casual acquaintance with Theban legend, and more than casual interest in the city's fate. There is of course a deliberate contrast to the passionately involved, even hysterical chorus of Theban women in the *Seven Against Thebes*, but as usual Euripides' purpose is not simply to be different from Aeschylus. His dramatic strategy calls for a chorus that can provide, with dispassionate authority, the long view of history as a guide to the meaning of the action. In the *parodos*, the Chorus explain that their final destination is not Thebes but Delphi, and then contrast that peaceful sanctuary with the war about to break out around them, setting the gleam of Dionysos' fires on the cliffs above Delphi against the baleful flames that light up Ares' cloud of war over Thebes. In the first *stasimon* they turn their thoughts to the founding of Thebes. Here too there is an underlying dichotomy, but now it resides entirely within Thebes. First there is the arrival of Kadmos, following the calf with which Apollo signaled his destination, a place all running streams and lush, fertile fields. Even the birth of Dionysos is fully subsumed into this peaceful idyll.[7] Then, suddenly, Ares' serpent is there, bloody and hostile, to guard the life-giving waters. Kadmos kills it and scatters its teeth in the soil; the soil gives birth to a race of armed men but immediately reclaims their bloodied corpses. Thus the foundation legend is a mixture of positive and negative symbols, the gentle calf and the wheat-bearing fields giving way inexorably to the fierce serpent and earth's crop of violent men.

The central contrast that we have observed in the *parodos* and first *stasimon* is extended in the second *stasimon* in a number of complex ways. The strophe again pits Ares against Dionysos, showing him in effect usurping and perverting the proper attributes of the Theban god. The antistrophe moves Theban saga forward to the birth of Oedipus and his conquest of the Sphinx. Here is at once a replication of Kadmos' slaying of the dragon and an implied identification of victor and vanquished. Both Oedipus and the Sphinx are creatures of the mountain; better that neither should have lived. The Sphinx shares Ares' attributes of hostility to the city and the perversion of the power of music; Oedipus gives birth to new strife in the form of his sons, whose birth is described as monstrous. The *epode* expresses the full complexity of the past the Chorus have been evoking: we return once more to the founding of Thebes, but this time the evocation of "the race sprung from the teeth of that / beast-eating, red-crested serpent" (951-52) yields to images of peace and productivity: the wedding of Harmonia, the rising of the city walls to Amphion's lyre, the birth of kings.

The beast in man is a recurrent theme in the later plays of Eu-

---

7. Appropriately, the Chorus, as they dance their tale in the orchestra, symbolize Dionysos' beneficence by his dancing with young Theban maidens, just as in the *parodos* their own dances in honor of the gods symbolize the order and harmony of Delphi.

ripides. The *Ion*, for example, images Kreousa, a descendant of earth-born Erecthonios and the bull-shaped Kephisos, as (in Ion's words) a "viper or serpent . . . no less venomous than the drops of Gorgon blood with which she tried to kill me." In the *Orestes*, the "beast-like spirit of murder that ever destroys our land and cities" (and has, in Tyndareus' eyes, already transformed Orestes into a serpent) fully brutalizes Orestes and Pylades. Menelaos, rushing to the burning palace where they have attempted to kill Helen and now hold Hermione at knife point, calls their acts "deeds of two lions—for I will not call them men." In the *Bacchae*, the equation of man and beast is far more extensive, and part of a terrifying abolition of all normal distinctions. Pentheus, for example, imprisons a bull that he imagines to be the priest of Dionysus; and his own mother, in her bacchic frenzy, mistakes him for a lion, strikes the first blow against him, and carries his head home on a stake, still thinking it a glorious hunting trophy. The same liminal confusion of man and beast pervades the *Phoenician Women*, but with the difference that here man's bestiality is paradoxically a productive as well as a destructive force. The sown-men offer the play's clearest paradigm of this duality. Sprung fully armed from the womb of Earth, on which Kadmos has scattered the teeth of a chthonian monster like seeds, they immediately engage each other in combat, drenching the ground with their blood. But ten survive to become the forebears of the Theban people.[8] Man's origin in the earth, his residual identity with the bestial, is the fertile source of his very life, but at the same time dooms him to bloodshed and violence.

The early history of Thebes, then, as it is developed in the choral lyrics of the *Phoenician Women* is a unity of opposites, a cycle of struggles between forces of creation and destruction which keep merging, changing form, reappearing, and which finally stand revealed at the heart of the dramatic action. In the words of Marilyn Arthur, "The monster and the monster-slayer each contain their own opposite, so that they are locked together in a cycle in which the hero becomes the city's bane, and the monster its savior."[9] Menoikeus' self-sacrifice becomes comprehensible as part of this cycle. Descended from the serpent's teeth, he is converted into the city's savior by becoming the serpent's prey. But the fatal duel of Polyneikes and Eteokles belongs

8. Similarly Io, the "horned maiden" whom Zeus turned into a heifer, pursued as far as Egypt, and made pregnant with the calf-child Epaphos, is repeatedly invoked as ancestor of the Phoenician, and thus the Theban, royal house.

9. *Op. cit.* (note 1, above), p. 173. How much this discussion owes to Professor Arthur's insights will be evident to anyone who has read her article.

to the cycle as well. Kadmos killed a monster and sowed its teeth as
the seeds of beastly creatures who died in brutal struggle. Oedipus
slew the Sphinx and sowed a beastly brood in his mother's womb, who
now destroy themselves. The third and fourth *stasima* reinforce this
sense of an inclusive and necessary circularity in the history of Thebes.
Immediately after Menoikeus' exit, the Chorus return to the Sphinx
and its monstrous ravaging of youths, and then naturally to Oedipus,
his monstrous marriage and accursed offspring. Only in the second
half of the antistrophe do they celebrate Menoikeus' heroism, but
their prayer to bear sons like him is addressed to Athena (1203-09),

> you who held
> the stone that slew
> the serpent, you who turned
> the mind of Kadmos
> to the deed from which
> all this devouring
> and destruction is derived!

Because so little is said, and so late, about Menoikeus, this ode has
been criticized since antiquity for its irrelevance. And yet it is the
clearest expression in the entire drama of the interconnectedness of
the bloodshed that marks Thebes' history.

With Menoikeus' death, the monster is appeased and Thebes
saved; but the circle is not yet closed, for the sons of Oedipus carry
the bestial element within them as an inheritance from their father.
The brief, almost breathless, final *stasimon* makes this clear by pic-
turing the foes as "twin beasts"; the messenger who reports their
fatal duel compares them (1513-14), as they charge at each other, to
"wild boars slashing with their tusks." The violence which began
when the city began and which is, as it were, the reverse of the coin
of order, cannot be escaped. This, not the traditional curse of Oedipus
construed as an isolated and willful act of wrath, is the agent of
fatality in the *Phoenician Women*. It is a pattern perpetuated ob-
sessively, but unwittingly. The more heroically, defiantly, autono-
mously, people seem to themselves to be acting, the more fully they
are participating in it. The elaborate nightmarelike symmetry of the
duel between the brothers, in which each blow is answered by an
equal counter-blow until the fated equilibrium of mutual slaughter
is reached, is perhaps the clearest example.[10] The juncture between

10. This symmetry is well brought out by R. Girard, *Violence and the Sacred*
(tr. P. Gregory, Baltimore, 1977), 44-45.

fatality and the apparently free and willful choice that is the main-spring of the dramatic action is thus necessarily and deeply ironic.

The play that results from so radical an irony is complex and defies facile judgments. Its range is extraordinary, even for Euripides. It might be compared with another play that flouts tradition, Shakespeare's *Troilus and Cressida*, in its ornate cynicism, hapless idealism, and underlying pessimism about human values. And yet, of course, that play is far less somber and far more bitter than this. One thing is certain: the *Phoenician Women* is not a failed tragedy of the Aristotelian or any other persuasion. It is an experiment on a grand scale, the work of a restless and daring mind.

V

The date of the *Phoenician Women* cannot be established with certainty, but the internal evidence of style and meter places it securely among Euripides' late plays. And there is helpful, although inconclusive, external evidence. The comment of a scholiast on Aristophanes, *Frogs* 53, strongly implies that our play is a few years later than Euripides' lost *Andromeda*, which we know to have been produced in 412 B.C. A *terminus ante quem* seems to be established by the poet's departure for Macedonia in 408 or 407. Thus the likeliest years for the production of the *Phoenician Women* are 409-407. An argument to the play by the grammarian Aristophanes, which unfortunately appears in a badly mutilated form of our manuscript tradition, can be interpreted to mean that the *Phoenician Women* was produced third in a tetralogy which began with *Oinomaios* and *Chrysippos* (plays which, like the *Phoenician Women*, presumably involved the working out of fatal curses), but this interpretation is by no means certain. Our play might also have been produced together with the extant *Orestes*, which we can date securely to 408.

The text of the *Phoenician Women* has not suffered more than most from the vagaries of manuscript transmission, but it shares with a few other plays (notably Aeschylus' *Seven Against Thebes*, which also shares its subject, and Euripides' own posthumously produced *Iphigeneia at Aulis*) the widespread suspicion that the author's text has been tampered with already in antiquity, and that in particular the exodos (which in the *Phoenician Women* is very long indeed) has suffered large-scale interpolation for later performance.[11] Any

11. This view has recently gained strong support from E. Fraenkel, *Zu den Phoenissen des Euripides, Sitzungsberichte der Bayerischen Akademie der Wissen-*

editor or translator must wrestle long and hard with this issue, made all the more complex by the fact that most of the suspect passages cannot simply be excised, since, if they are indeed interpolated, they must have supplanted genuine passages necessary for the advancement of the plot. Our approach, after some vacillation, has been to excise only such lines as seemed to us indefensibly otiose or nonsensical (in truth, no more than one might excise in many another play of Euripides), even though this means retaining material about which we have strong reservations. Our only substantial cut is from line 1737 (Greek text) to the end, where we are inclined to accept Wilamowitz's view that the received text preserves a spurious doublet to 1710-36. Feeling that our readers have a right to know what we have chosen to omit, we offer plain prose versions and brief rationales for each of our cuts in the Notes on the Text. The reader will also find there some indication of our doubts concerning passages· we have chosen to retain.

The text upon which this translation is based is an eclectic one, most closely resembling that of A. C. Pearson (Cambridge, 1909), from whose annotations we have also derived much help.

VI

As for the translation, it will speak for itself, but a few general comments may help orient the reader to our procedures. We have not aimed at a thoroughly "vernacular" version. The play is at once close and remote, colloquial and brocaded in expression and texture. Its characters are rulers, its rhetoric formal, its encounters stylized; and yet its multiple layers of irony, its constant shifts of tonality, keep undercutting the "heroic" matrix, the comfortable or expected response.

Greek tragic texts are libretti (as the creators of opera in late sixteenth-century Florence were quick to understand), verbal tokens of a total theatrical experience wedded to music and dance, to the visual cues of masking and costume convention, gesture, and movement in theatrical space. Much of this experience is forever lost, but the translator who does not try to conjure it up in his mind's eye and ear will never be fully in touch with the text. We have tried to make

---

schaften, Philosophisch-Historische Klasse, 1963, Heft 1 (Munich, 1963). Further discussion by H. Diller, *Gnomon* 36 (1964), 641-50; H. Erbse, *Philologus* 110 (1966), 1-110; M. Reeves, *Greek, Roman, and Byzantine Studies* 13 (1972), 541-74; D. J. Mastronarde, "Studies in Euripides' Phoinissai" (diss., Toronto, 1974); M. W. Haslam, *Classical Quarterly* 26 (1976), 4-10.

our version an enactment, speakable (in the case of the choral lyrics, one might say "danceable"), capable of being performed as well as read. It would be our greatest reward to see it reach sympathetic production, for drama, especially Greek drama, lives fully only in the theater.

If, as has been said, "The translator of poetry walks a tightrope across an abyss,"[12] one might suppose that collaborative translators, each tugging at the other to pull him a little closer to his own position, would run a special risk of disastrous falls. We can only say that this has not been our experience. Each has helped the other to keep his balance whenever he seemed to be bending back too far in the direction of philology, or leaning out too far toward poetic fancy. Ours has been, from the beginning, a genuine collaboration, although conducted by correspondence, sometimes between continents, and not without depressions, doubts, and delays as we strove toward a mutual understanding of Euripides' complex, often paradoxical conception. We are grateful to the General Editor for his careful guidance in our final stages as well as his unfailing encouragement throughout, and not least for his patience.

Durham, North Carolina　　　　　　　　　PETER BURIAN
New York City　　　　　　　　　　　　　BRIAN SWANN
March 1980

12. John L. Foster, "On Translating Hieroglyphic Love Songs," in S. Baker, ed., *The Essayist* (New York, 1977), 128.

THE PHOENICIAN WOMEN

CHARACTERS

OEDIPUS son of Laios and Jokasta, once king of Thebes
JOKASTA Oedipus' mother and wife
POLYNEIKES son of Oedipus and Jokasta, exiled by Eteokles
ETEOKLES Polyneikes' brother, ruling in Thebes
ANTIGONE daughter of Oedipus and Jokasta
TUTOR of Antigone
KREON brother of Jokasta
MENOIKEUS son of Kreon
TEIRESIAS the prophet
MESSENGER
CHORUS of Phoenician maidens

Line numbers in the right-hand margin refer to the English translation only, and the Notes at p. 87 are keyed to these lines. The bracketed line numbers in the running headlines refer to the Greek text.

The scene is Thebes. The stage building, with its central double doors, repre-
sents the royal palace. JOKASTA, *unattended and dressed all in black, her hair*
close-cropped as a sign of mourning, enters through the central doors.

JOKASTA Sun, flaring in your flames, what a harmful ray
you hurled at Thebes that day when Kadmos quit
seaswept Phoenicia, and came to this country.
Here he married Harmonia, child of Kypris. His son
Polydoros fathered Labdakos, father of Laios.
Men know me as Menoikeus' child.
My father called me Jokasta. Laios married me,
but after a long marriage with no children
he drove to Delphi, to petition Apollo for
the children he craved for his house. But the god replied: 10
"Lord of horse-rich Thebes, do not fling your seed
into the furrow, flouting the gods. If you make
a son you make your own murderer. Your whole line
will wade through blood." Yet Laios did succumb to lust.
Flush with liquor, he planted a seed in me.
Then, seeing his mistake, and recalling the god's words,
he gave the child to cowherds to discard
in the meadow of Hera under the scaur
of Kithairon, first inserted spikes of iron
through his ankles. Hence the name "Oedipus,"   20
"Swell-foot," by which Greece came to know him.
But the men who minded Polybos' horses
carried this child to their chief, and laid him in
their mistress' lap. She received the result of my birthpangs,
put it to her breast, and persuaded her lord
she'd borne a boy. Later, when his first beard
had begun to bloom, either having thought things out
for himself, or having heard the gossip, my son
departed for Delphi to discover his true parents'

identity. Laios my husband also left   30
for Delphi, to see if the son he abandoned were alive
or dead. Together they reached the same spot, the split
in the Phokis road, and Laios' driver roared:
"Out of the road, stranger! Make way for a king!"
But he walked on, proud, without a word,
though the horses with their hoofs bloodied the tendons
of his feet. Then followed—but why not steer straight
to the point? Son killed father; took chariot and team
to bring to Polybos, who brought him up. But when
the Sphinx ravaged the city with her raids, and my husband   40
had died, my brother Kreon made it known that my bed
was the prize for the person who unraveled the subtle
maiden's riddle. And somehow it happened that Oedipus
my son understood the Sphinx's song, and took
the scepter of this country as reward, and took
as bride her who bore him, the miserable man—
and she who bore him did not know she was
sleeping with her son. So to my child I gave birth
to two children, two males, Eteokles
and Polyneikes the powerful, and two females,   50
one her father called Ismene, the other
I called Antigone. Then, when he realized
that marrying me he had married his mother, this
Oedipus who sustained all sufferings
struck slaughter into his eyes, bloodying the pupils
with clasps of beaten gold. And when my sons'
cheeks were clouded with beard, they buried their father
behind bolted doors, hoping fate might be forgotten,
a fate that needed too much clever contrivance
to explain away. He is alive, in his lodging,   60
suffering his fate. He curses his sons
with the unholiest curses: prays they split their patrimony
with sharp steel. They fell to fearing the gods
would make his prayers flower, if they lived together,
and made up their minds that the younger, Polyneikes,
would be the first to leave this land in voluntary exile,
while Eteokles would stay to wield the scepter,

and year by year they'd exchange rule. But when
Eteokles enjoyed the helmsman's bench
he held to it tight. He took up all the throne   70
and exiled Polyneikes from this land.
When Polyneikes arrived in Argos, he made
Adrastos his relative by marriage, and mustered a great
army of Argives with himself at the head. And now
he stands against these seven-gated walls
claiming his father's scepter and his share
in the land. But to cure this strife I have caused
son to come to son by a truce, before
they use their spears. The courier I sent
says Polyneikes will come. But you who sit   80
in the shining folds of sky, Zeus, save us!
Reconcile my children. Your wisdom should not allow
the same man to be mastered by misfortune forever.

JOKASTA *returns to the palace. The old* TUTOR *appears on the
roof of the stage building, followed by* ANTIGONE, *who remains at first on the ladder behind the stage building, only
                                          partly exposed to view.*

TUTOR Antigone, your father's green branch, glory
of his house, since your mother lets you
leave the women's quarters for the highest
part of the palace, to scan the Argive spears
as you had begged, stay here while I survey
the path in case there's someone walking there
below. If we are seen, it could rain reproach   90
on me, a slave, and touch you too, a queen.
But I'll tell you everything I know, everything
I saw and heard when I took the wine
of truce to your brother, and brought his tokens back.

At the front of the roof, looking around.

No, there's no one near the palace. Climb
these old cedar steps and look at the plain.

See the huge army of your enemies encamped
along the banks of Ismenos' stream, and Dirke's.

ANTIGONE   Stretch, yes stretch an old hand
to a young hand,   100
and help me lift my feet
from the ladder.

TUTOR   Hold my hand, lady. You've come at the crucial moment.
The Argive army's on the move. It has just now decamped.
They're dividing the companies one from another.

ANTIGONE   Ah, lady, daughter of Leto,
Hekate,
the whole field
flashes with bronze!

TUTOR   Well, Polyneikes has not just come for a visit,   110
but in high blood, with many horsemen.

ANTIGONE   The gates, with their bolts
and the brass-bound portcullis
before the walls that Amphion
made with music, do they
hold fast?

TUTOR   Be brave!
Inside at least the city is safe.
But look at the fighter out in front!   120

ANTIGONE   Who is he, that captain
with a white crest
leading his men,
lifting high on his arm
the bronze shield?

TUTOR   One of their captains, lady.

ANTIGONE But who? Where's he from?
          Tell me, old man,
          what do men call him?

TUTOR   Hippomedon. He boasts of Mycenaean birth
          and lives by Lerna's stream.   130

ANTIGONE Oh, how arrogant he looks,
          how horrible to look at!
          Just like an earth-born giant in pictures,
          star-bright,
          not like our mortal species.

TUTOR   Can you make out that man crossing the waters of Dirke?

ANTIGONE Another kind again,
          his armor
          a contrast.
          Who is he?   140

TUTOR   Tydeus, son of Oineus, from Aitolia.
          A man warlike as their Ares.

ANTIGONE Old friend, is this the man
          who married the sister
          of Polyneikes' wife?
          How outlandish his dress,
          half-foreign!

TUTOR   Yes, all the Aitolians carry large leather shields, child,
          and throw their javelins more skilfully than anyone.

ANTIGONE How are you so familiar with these facts?   150

TUTOR   I remember the signs I saw on their shields.

ANTIGONE Who is that passing
          by the monument of Zethos,

25

that youth with the long wavy hair
and a fierce look on his face?
A captain, for behind him
on foot, his men crowd round
in full armor.

TUTOR That is Atalanta's son, Parthenopaios.

ANTIGONE I ask Artemis,   160
who roams the hills
with his mother,
to tame him with arrows
since he comes to my city
to sack it.

TUTOR But they have justice on their side,
which I'm afraid the gods will see.

ANTIGONE Where is he,
born of the same mother as me,
to a fate of much suffering?   170
Wise old man,
tell me the whereabouts of Polyneikes.

TUTOR He stands beside Adrastos, by the tomb
of Niobe's seven daughters. Do you see?

ANTIGONE I can see, but not clearly.
I see a kind of silhouette,
the cast of his profile.
If only I could fly,
a windblown cloud
through the air to my brother. . . .   180
If only I could throw my arms at last
around the dear neck
of the unhappy exile!
How glorious he looks
in his gold armor,
old man!
He is gleaming like dawn's darts!

TUTOR He will soon be here at the palace under a truce,
to fill you with happiness.

ANTIGONE But old friend, who's the man   190
mounted in a chariot,
holding the reins
of white horses?

TUTOR Amphiaraos, mistress, the seer. And with him
victims for sacrifice, brought to shed
welcome blood for the earth.

ANTIGONE Oh, daughter of Leto, dressed
all in light,
Selanaia,
gold circle of sheen—
his goad is so calm and controlled   200
as he taps
each of his horses in turn!
But where is the man who
with brute arrogant blasts
batters our city?

TUTOR Kapaneus? There, sizing up the towers
for the right place to put his scaling-ladders.

ANTIGONE Ah, Nemesis, and deep-swelling thunder of Zeus,
smoky light of the lightning, it is for you
to put his proud boasting to sleep!   210
He is the man who said he would seize
the women of Thebes and
hand them over to the households
of Mycenae
and the trident
of Lerna:
enslave them to the spring
Poseidon's trident struck
from the rock
at Lerna   220

for love of the nymph
Amymone.
O Artemis, golden-haired daughter of Zeus,
save me from slavery!

TUTOR Child, go back inside the house and stay
in the cover of your women's quarters, for you
have satisfied your wish, you have seen
what you wanted to see. The city's in confusion.
A crowd of women's running toward the palace.
And women are quick to find fault. Once they've chosen   230
a target, they launch the attack, and bring up
        reinforcements.
It gives women some sort of pleasure to say
nothing good about one another.

Exit ANTIGONE *by the ladder behind the stage-building, fol-*
lowed by the TUTOR. *As they disappear from view, the*
CHORUS *of Phoenician captive girls enter the orchestra,*
                                                        singing.

CHORUS Leaving Tyrian foam,
        I have come as firstfruits for Apollo
from the island of Phoenicia,
        a slave for the dwelling of Phoibos
under the snow-locked ledges of Parnassos.
        Oars hauled me over
Ionian seas   240
        whose fruitless plains flow
round Sicily.
                Since Zephyros
spurred his breezes
        the sky
                was filled
                        with a lovely
                                rushing
                                        of
                                                air.   250

28

Chosen for Loxias
   as loveliest prize of my city,
I was carried to Kadmos' land,
   to the towers of Laios that are
kin to the glorious line
   of Agenor.
I have become a handmaid of Phoibos,
   dedicated like a gold votive offering.
But still the waters of Kastalia
   wait for me to wash   260
in the service of Phoibos
   the splendor of my virginity,
my hair.

O rock,
   flashing with the flare
of tossing torches over
   the frenzied heights of Dionysos,
and you vine that daily
   let drop
the many-globed grapecluster   270
   as you send out shoots;
O cave, you cave of the serpent
   Apollo slew,
you sacred mountains scattered with snow,

                    let me leave
                    Dirke's stream

     and dance
         to honor you deities,
     become the daring dancer of the god
       beside the inner cavern and Earth's navel!   280
But now I see before the walls
   Ares berserk, kindling blood
to blaze against this city—
   oh, stop him!
The griefs of kin are held in common,
   and Phoenicia suffers too
if this town of the seven towers

suffers in any way.
Shared blood, shared children
   were born of   290
horn-bearing Io.
   I have a share in this suffering.

Around the city
   a black cloud of shields
bursts into blood-red
   flames of battle
which Ares will soon assess,
   bringing to the children of Oedipus
evil from the Erinyes.
   O Pelasgian Argos,   300
I am afraid of your power,
   and the gods'. Not without right
the man who comes against our country
   flings himself into this furor.

Enter POLYNEIKES *from the left, looking warily about him*
              as he proceeds toward the palace doors.

POLYNEIKES The gatekeeper's locks have let me inside the walls,
which makes me fear that once my feet are in
the snare, the Thebans won't let me out unbloodied.
I must keep my eyes open, watchful this way and that
for a trick. My hand is heavy with this sword: I shall
collect proof of my courage.
                           Ha! Who's this? Or does   310
a shadow scare me? Everything seems startling
to the man who takes risks, whenever his soles touch
enemy soil. My mother, who got me here
under a truce—I trust her. And I do not
trust her. But a bulwark looms near. Close by are
hearths for sacrifice, and the palace is
not empty. Here, I'll drive my sword into
its dark scabbard, and demand from these women near
the house who they are.

                   Foreign ladies, tell me,
from what land did you set sail for the palaces of Greece?   320

CHORUS Phoenicia was the land that reared me. But Agenor's
LEADER grandchildren have sent me here as firstfruits
       of battle for Phoibos. The famous son of Oedipus
       wanted to send me on to the awesome oracle
       of Loxias, and to his hearth. But at
       that instant, the Argives sent their arms against
       the city.
               And now you answer me. Who are you,
       traveling to Thebes and its seven towers?

POLYNEIKES Oedipus is my father, son of Laios.
       Jokasta, child of Menoikeus, is my mother.   330
       The Theban people call me Polyneikes.

CHORUS O kin of Agenor's sons,
          my lords, by whom I am banished,
       I fall to my knees before you, master,
          honoring the customs of my home.
       In time's long turning
          you've returned to your land.
       Mistress, mistress! Come quickly from the house!
          Throw the doors open!
       Do you hear, mother who bore him?   340
          Why do you take so long to leave the house
       and hold your son in your arms?

                  Enter JOKASTA *from the palace.*

JOKASTA Your Phoenician cry I heard, girls,
       and I drag my old legs with shaking steps.
       Ah, child, at last, after countless days!
       Come to your mother's breast,
       bring your cheeks to mine!
       Let your dark curls fall over my face!
       Ah, you have arrived unexpected,

unhoped for,   350
into your mother's arms!
What shall I say? With hands and words,
or dancing in the whirl of joy,
I can relive the old delight!
Ah, child, you left your father's land
in desolation, banished
by a shameless brother,
yearned for by your friends,
yearned for by Thebes.
That is why I keep my white hair short.   360
Weeping, I let it grow unkempt
in my grief.
I am not wearing white robes, son.
In their place I've wrapped around me
these black rags.
The blind old man in the palace,
ever since the like-feathered pair of you
slipped the jesses of home,
persists in his intent
to kill himself,   370
seeking the sword
and the noose to toss over the beam.
He curses his children, and with
loud continual cries
hides himself in the gloom.
But you, my son, I hear have married,
and have the pleasure of making children
in a foreigner's mansion. You cherish
a foreign kinship—misery
for your mother, for Laios,   380
and his long-famed race
is the ruin of an alien marriage.
I did not light the torch,
as is the happy mother's custom
when a son marries.
The river Ismenos was deprived
of his share in the solemnities,

the pleasure of providing the water,
when you went ahead with your wedding.
Throughout the city of Thebes   390
the entrance of your bride was silent.
Curse these griefs, whether caused by war
or quarrels or your father
or the fate that's held revel
in Oedipus' house!
Upon me the weight of the evil is fallen.

CHORUS   The pangs of childbirth are frightening and painful
LEADER   for women. And so all women worship their children.

POLYNEIKES   Mother, after careful thought, I have come
carelessly among my enemies. But no one   400
can choose not to love his native soil.
He who says otherwise loves words, not truth.
I was so frightened, I came in such fear that some ruse
of my brother would ruin me, that I walked through this city
clutching my sword, turning my head this way and that.
Only one thing gave me comfort: your truce, and your pledge
that let me pass through ancestral walls. I came
weeping, seeing after so long the seats and altars
of the gods, the gymnasia where I was reared,
the waters of Dirke. I have been exiled from these,   410
living in a strange land, my eyes streaming tears—
but I go from one grief to another. I see you,
your hair cropped close, dressed in black robes.
O, my sorrows! How strange and monstrous, mother,
is hatred within families.

JOKASTA   It is wrong for one of the gods to destroy the family
of Oedipus. And it all began when your father
wrongly married me and made you.
It all began when I gave birth. But what
can be done? We have to endure what the gods give.   420
Without hurting you, I don't know how to ask
what I want to know. And yet I'm forced to ask.

POLYNEIKES Ask. Ask anything you want. Whatever
you want, mother, is dear to me.

JOKASTA Well then, I'll ask this first. What is it like
to lose one's native land? Is it great loss?

POLYNEIKES The worst loss of all. Words can't describe it.

JOKASTA But what's it really like? Why is exile so hard?

POLYNEIKES Because a man's tongue is not free.

JOKASTA Not speak freely? A slave's life!   430

POLYNEIKES You must endure the arrogance of power.

JOKASTA Too painful! To share the folly of fools!

POLYNEIKES You have to violate your nature.
You live a slave's life to survive.

JOKASTA But exiles live on hope, or so the saying goes.

POLYNEIKES Hope's lovely to look at, but lives in the future.

JOKASTA And doesn't time say plainly hopes are vain?

POLYNEIKES In time of trouble, hoping
has a sort of charm.

JOKASTA How did you find food before you married money?   440

POLYNEIKES Some days I had enough. Others, nothing.

JOKASTA Your father's friends, didn't they help?

POLYNEIKES You'd better be a success!
Misfortune has no friends.

JOKASTA But surely your high birth helped you to rise?

POLYNEIKES Not having hurts. You can't eat rank.

JOKASTA A man's country is the dearest thing he has.

POLYNEIKES Too dear for words to say.

JOKASTA How did you get to Argos? What was your plan?

POLYNEIKES I don't know. The god summoned me to my fate.   450

JOKASTA The god is wise. How did you happen to marry?

POLYNEIKES The prophecy of Apollo. The god spoke to Adrastos.

JOKASTA What did you say? I don't understand.

POLYNEIKES He prophesied that Adrastos' daughters
would marry a lion and a boar.

JOKASTA What do you have to do with these wild animals, son?

POLYNEIKES It was night.
I came to Adrastos' door.

JOKASTA A wandering exile, looking for a bed?

POLYNEIKES Yes. Then someone else arrived.   460
An exile like me.

JOKASTA Poor man. Who was he?

POLYNEIKES Tydeus, son of Oineus.

JOKASTA Why did Adrastos think you were wild beasts?

POLYNEIKES We fought over a bed.

JOKASTA And that was when Adrastos understood the oracle?

POLYNEIKES And gave us both his daughters in marriage.

JOKASTA Was your marriage a happy one?

POLYNEIKES Happy to this day. I have no complaints.

JOKASTA How did you recruit the army   470
      you led against Thebes?

POLYNEIKES Adrastos swore to his new sons-in-law
      he would repatriate us both, me first.
      And many chief men of the Danaans and Mycenaeans
      are here, doing me a painful favor, but
      a necessary one. For I'm leading an army
      against my own city—I swear by the gods that I
      go to war with no relish against relatives
      only too willing to fight. But unraveling
      these wrongs lies in your hands, Mother; to   480
      reconcile kin again, thus saving me,
      yourself, and the whole city from suffering
      and grief. It may be trite, but I still say:
      "Properties and money are a man's best friend,
      and have the greatest influence in the end."
      So with ten thousand men I come to look
      for them. A beggar is no nobleman.

CHORUS Here's Eteokles now, coming to
LEADER this reconciliation. Jokasta, as
      their mother you must say what you can   490
      to reconcile your sons.

      Enter ETEOKLES *from the right. In dress and general appear-*
      ance he closely resembles POLYNEIKES, *but his entrance is as*
      swift and imperious as his brother's was hesitant and skittish.
      He is attended by a small retinue of unarmed servants.

ETEOKLES   Mother, I've come. I'm here as a favor to you.
            What's all this about? Someone had better
            start explaining. I've halted my work
            of mustering the citizens about the walls
            and setting ambushes for chariots in order
            to hear your impartial arbitration—that's why
            I agreed to your request to allow this fellow
            here inside our walls under a truce.

JOKASTA   Enough, Eteokles! Haste brings no justice.   500
            Slow speech achieves the greatest wisdom.
            Calm your angry eye and outbursts of anger.
            You are not glaring at some gorgon's head,
            severed at the throat. This is your brother.
                          —And you, Polyneikes,
            look at your brother. If you look him
            in the eye, you will speak softer; you
            will hear him better. I have some sound advice
            to give you both. When kinsmen and brothers are angry
            with each other, let each look the other squarely   510
            in the eye. Let both keep in mind the purpose
            of their meeting, and forget old grievances.
            Polyneikes, you speak first. You come
            with your Argive army, claiming to be wronged.
            Now may some god reconcile your grievances!

POLYNEIKES Truth is single by nature, and what is right
            needs no many-colored gloss. It has
            its own right measure. But the unjust argument,
            unhealthy, diseased, needs the medicine   520
            of clever words. I looked forward to
            my share, as he to his, in our inheritance,
            hoping to escape the curses which
            our father Oedipus heaped on our heads
            long ago. I myself, of my own
            free will, renounced this land, yielding it
            into his hands for one year's circle, with
            the intent of ruling in my turn. In

this way I hoped to avoid envy and hate,
by not doing wrong and then suffering it in turn—
but this is what's happened: he who swore by the gods   530
with solemn oaths kept no part of his promise.
Instead, he clings to power and keeps my share
in this state.
        Even now I am prepared,
on condition that I get what's mine, to send
my army away from Thebes, and to take charge
of my own house, turn and turn about,
and then to transfer it back to him at the end
of my year. I will not plunder my own city.
I will not set my scaling ladders against
this city's walls—not unless justice is   540
denied me. And I summon the gods to witness that,
though I myself have acted justly, my country
has been stolen from me, wickedly, impiously.
This is how things stand, Mother, stated
simply, without the entanglements of words.
It takes no great intelligence to see
that I have spoken justly—or so it seems to me.

CHORUS Although I am not Greek, what you have said
LEADER seems sensible and right.

ETEOKLES If all men agreed on what is wise and just,   550
there'd be no argument, no strife. But now,
nothing is like or equal, except in name.
The *fact* is something else again.
               Mother,
I'll tell you plainly without pretense, I'd run
to the rising of the sun, I'd go beneath
the earth, if I could have absolute power,
the greatest god of all. Power is *good*,
Mother. I will not give it up. I want it
for myself. It would be cowardice
to lose the great good thing and settle for   560
the less. Besides, I'm ashamed to think that he

should achieve his ends by coming here with arms
to sack this city. What disgrace for Thebes
if, for fear of Mycenaean spears,
I surrender my scepter to him. He had no right
to come here with arms to seek a settlement.
Reason can accomplish everything
that enemy steel can do. So, if he wants
to stay here on some other terms, I'll grant it.
But I will not yield to his demands. Now I   570
can rule alone I will not be a slave
to him.
    So, send out fire, unsheathe
swords, harness horses, fill the plain
with chariots! I will not part with power!
This one thing makes wrong right: power.
In other things I'm all for virtue.

CHORUS You should not praise such actions.
LEADER They are not noble.
    Justice cannot tolerate them.

JOKASTA My son, there's more to old age than misery.   580
    Experience sometimes speaks more wisely than
the young. Why pursue the worst of gods,
Ambition? Let her be, my son, she is
an evil goddess. To many houses and happy
cities she has come and gone, leaving
wreckage in her wake. And *this* is the goddess
you go wild for! Wiser, child, to honor
Equality, who binds kin to kin, city
to city, ally to ally. Equality
is man's natural law, but the Less is always   590
fighting against the More—so dawns the day
of hate. And Equality established our numbers.
Equality made measures and weights for man.
The lightless eye of the night and the light of the sun
move equal through the cycle of the year.
Each one yields, neither resents the other.

So sun and night are slaves for mortal men.
But you cannot accept an equal share
in your own house, and consign his share to him?
Where's the justice in that? Why praise power,   600
that injustice which you call happiness? Why
exaggerate its importance? No! It's empty!
Or do you hope to pile up wealth—and its wealth
of trouble? What is this "more"? Always "more"?
Just a word. For the wise man sufficient
is enough.
        Come, let me ask you. Which
do you really prefer: to stay in power, or save
your city? Is your answer power? But what
if Polyneikes conquers you; if Argive spears
conquer the Kadmean? Will you see   610
your Theban city shattered, most of its women
taken captive, raped by enemy soldiers?
Then Thebes will reap only grief for this wealth
you chase in the name of your ambition.
So much for you.
        Now, Polyneikes, I speak
to you. This favor Adrastos did you was
sheer folly, and you were mad to attempt the sack
of Thebes. Suppose you do lay waste this city—
which heaven forbid! What trophies can you dedicate
to Zeus? And how will you start the sacrifice   620
to celebrate destroying your own country?
How will you inscribe the shields you place
along the banks of the Inachos?
"When Polyneikes had sacked Thebes, he set
these shields up in honor of the gods"?
Never let that be your fame in Hellas, son!
But suppose that you are beaten. Suppose his army
conquers yours. How then can you return
to Argos, leaving thousands of corpses behind?
Some Argive is certain to say: "Adrastos, what   630
disaster you've brought on us with this bridegroom.
In one girl's marriage all Argos has been ruined."

40

Two evils then face you, child: if you fail
at Thebes, you lose Argos also. Tame
your excesses, both of you! When twin follies
converge, the result's disaster!

CHORUS O gods, bring this mischief to an end.
LEADER Make the sons of Oedipus agree again.

ETEOKLES Mother, the war is words no more. This meeting
was wasted. Your goodwill has brought us nothing.   640
We could never come together except on my terms:
that I keep my power and rule this kingdom.
Spare your tedious cautions! Let me go!
(to POLYNEIKES) And you—clear out or die!

POLYNEIKES At whose hands? Show me the man who's
swordsman enough to kill me, and not die himself!

ETEOKLES Open your eyes. I am that man.
Do you see these hands, and this sword?

POLYNEIKES What I see is a rich man.
A coward clinging to life.   650

ETEOKLES And you have to bring so many men
to make this cowardly nothing kneel?

POLYNEIKES A careful captain's better than a rash one.

ETEOKLES Loudmouth! You trust the truce to save you—

POLYNEIKES It saves you too! A second time I claim
the scepter and my share.

ETEOKLES And again we reject your claim.
My house is mine. I'll keep it mine.

POLYNEIKES Taking more than your share?

ETEOKLES Yes. Now get out! 660

POLYNEIKES O altars of my ancestral gods—

ETEOKLES Which you plan to plunder.

POLYNEIKES Hear me!

ETEOKLES Who are you calling? What god will listen to
a man who fights his own country?

POLYNEIKES O homes of our gods, gods of the white horses—

ETEOKLES Who hate you.

POLYNEIKES I have been driven from my country—

ETEOKLES Which you have come to destroy.

POLYNEIKES Unjustly, O gods! 670

ETEOKLES Call on the gods of Mycenae, not Thebes.

POLYNEIKES You have no gods!

ETEOKLES I'm not my country's enemy, like you.

POLYNEIKES You chased me off and took my share.

ETEOKLES Yes—and I'll take your life too.

POLYNEIKES O father, do you see my sufferings?

ETEOKLES He also sees what you're up to.

POLYNEIKES And you, Mother?

ETEOKLES On your lips, that name is obscene.

POLYNEIKES O city of Thebes!

ETEOKLES Clear off to Argos! Go call
on the waters of Lerna!

POLYNEIKES Don't worry. I'm leaving.
I'm grateful to you, Mother.

ETEOKLES Get out! Get out of this land!

POLYNEIKES I'm leaving. But let me see my father first.

ETEOKLES Not a chance.

POLYNEIKES Then let me see my sisters.

ETEOKLES You'll never see them again.

POLYNEIKES Oh, my sisters!   690

ETEOKLES Why call for your sisters?
You're their worst enemy.

POLYNEIKES Mother, goodbye.

JOKASTA Goodbye! You see what good is left me!

POLYNEIKES You have lost your son.

JOKASTA I was born to suffering and sorrow.

POLYNEIKES This man insults my very nature.

ETEOKLES I have returned him insult for insult.

POLYNEIKES Where will you fight? By which tower?

ETEOKLES What's it to you?   700

POLYNEIKES To take my position opposite,
and kill you.

ETEOKLES I plan exactly the same for you.

JOKASTA No, my sons!
For god's sake, what are you doing?

POLYNEIKES You'll soon see.

JOKASTA Won't you try to escape your father's curses?

ETEOKLES Let the whole house fall to ruin!

POLYNEIKES My bloodstained sword will be lazy no longer!
I call the gods as witnesses, and the land   710
that weaned me, that dishonored, insulted, I am
driven from my country like a slave,
as though I were not just as much my father's
son as he. And so, Thebes, for the fate
you suffer, lay the blame on him, not me.
I marched to Thebes against my will. Against
my will I was driven out. Apollo, lord
of the roadways, O house that sheltered me,
farewell! And you, friends of my youth, and you
honey-laden altars of the gods.   720
I do not know if I shall ever speak
to you again. But my hopes are not asleep.
I still believe that with the help of heaven
I'll conquer him and win this kingdom back.

ETEOKLES For the final time—get out! How right that our father,
with divine foreknowledge, named you "Polyneikes,"
since "discord" is what you are.

JOKASTA *enters the palace, and* POLYNEIKES *exits on the left.*
ETEOKLES *and his attendants retire to the right side of the*
stage, where they remain motionless during the choral song.

CHORUS Kadmos came from Tyre
    to this land where
a wild calf fell   730
    to its knees,
thus fulfilling
    the divine oracle
that directed Kadmos to settle
    the wheat-thick plains
where from lovely river water
    the moisture sinks in its fullness
into Dirke's green and
    deep-sown ground.
Here a mother bore Bromios,   740
    son of Zeus,
over whom twisting ivy
    sent its tendrils
tipped with green,
    covering him in its leafy shade
while he was still a baby,
    to make him smile.
Dionysos, partner in dances
    of young Theban girls
and women who raise   750
    "Evoé"
for him.

Here slid the gory snake
    whose pupils darted
from place to place;
    the savage guard of Ares' spring
and streams that make
    the land grow green.
While fetching lustral waters,
    Kadmos killed him,   760
blow upon blow to his brute head
    from the crystal rock
he held tight
    in his monster-killing fist.

At the order of the heavenly
   unmothered one, Pallas Athene,
Kadmos scattered the great snake's teeth
   and they fell into the furrows
of rich fields.
   Then through the surface of her soil   770
Earth erupted the likeness
   of armed men.
Slaughter with a soul of iron
   drew them down again to bare earth
and soaked in blood the soil
   that had shown them to the sunlit
breezes of upper air.

I invoke you, Epaphos,
   offspring long ago of our ancestor
Io, and offspring of Zeus.   780
   I call on you with foreign cries,
ah, with foreign prayers.
   Come, come to this city
founded by your descendants
   and devoted to the goddesses
we name in the same breath:
   Persephone and dear Demeter,
ruler of all things,
   nurse of all things,
Earth Mother.   790

Epaphos,
   look after this land
and send the goddesses with torches
   held high in their hands.
To the gods who sit in power
   everything is easy.

ETEOKLES (*to an attendant*) You, stir yourself, and bring back Kreon,
son of Menoikeus, brother of my mother
Jokasta. Tell him this: I want to talk

with him on domestic matters, and things that touch   800
the common good before I take my place
among the spears and start the battle. No, wait.

Enter KREON *from the left*

He saves you trouble by coming here himself.

KREON I've been looking for you everywhere, my lord
Eteokles. I've searched all the gates and guard-posts
in Thebes, trying to find you.

ETEOKLES I wanted to see you too. When Polyneikes and I
met to parley, I saw there'd be no reconciliation.

KREON I've heard he has great things in store for Thebes,
thanks to his alliance with Adrastos,   810
and his army. But all this is in the gods' hands.
I've come to tell you of a dangerous new development.

ETEOKLES What new development?

KREON We've captured an Argive soldier.

ETEOKLES What's he say they're up to now?

KREON Their army is about to surround Thebes.

ETEOKLES Then Thebes must answer, and meet them in the field!

KREON In the field? This is youthful brashness!

ETEOKLES Beyond the trenches. That's where we'll meet them.

KREON We're few. They're many.   820

ETEOKLES I know they're powerful—at boasting.

KREON Among Greeks, Argos has a great reputation.

ETEOKLES Take courage! I'll pile the plain high with their corpses!

KREON I hope so. But a great effort will be needed.

ETEOKLES And that way, I won't keep my men cooped up inside
the city.

KREON But victory comes from good advice.

ETEOKLES You advise me then to take a different road?

KREON Try them all. You can get trapped in one.

ETEOKLES A night-attack, perhaps? Surprise them by ambush?

KREON Good. Provided you can get home safely.   830

ETEOKLES Night's neutral, but it favors the bold.

KREON If things miscarry, darkness can bring disaster.

ETEOKLES What if we attacked when they were eating?

KREON There'd be some panic, but victory's what we need.

ETEOKLES If they retreat, they'll have to cross
the Dirke ford. And it's too deep.

KREON It's a good idea to proceed with caution.

ETEOKLES What about a frontal attack? With cavalry?

KREON They're in strong positions, protected by chariots.

ETEOKLES What's left then? Do I surrender Thebes?   840

KREON Of course not! Think. You're a clever man.

ETEOKLES Can you propose a better plan than mine?

KREON I've heard them say seven men have been chosen . . .

ETEOKLES Seven men? Seven's no great number.

KREON Each of the seven will lead a company
to assault each of our seven gates.

ETEOKLES What should we do? Not just sit and wait!

KREON Appoint seven men of your own, one to each gate.

ETEOKLES For single combat, or in command of troops?

KREON Commanders of the bravest troops you have. 850

ETEOKLES I see. To keep the walls from being scaled.

KREON Assign them adjutants. One man can't see everything.

ETEOKLES Chosen for courage or intelligence?

KREON Both. One's worthless without the other.

ETEOKLES Agreed! I'll go to the seven gates and station
commanders there, as you suggest. I'll pit
seven men of mine against their seven.
But there's no time now to name each commander,
not with their army camped right under our walls.
I'm on my way. We must get moving. With luck 860
I'll find my brother opposite me. I'll take him
prisoner, or kill him for coming to destroy my city.
But if I fail, it's up to you, Kreon,
to arrange the marriage of my sister Antigone
to your son Haimon. Here and now, before
I leave, I confirm the agreement for betrothal
which we made before. You are my mother's brother,
so I hardly need to say: Take good care of her,
for your sake and mine. When my father put out

49

his eyes, he proved himself a fool. I cannot   870
praise him, for he knew that his curses
might kill us.
                    One thing is still undone:
we must know if Teiresias has some guidance
for us. I'll send your son Menoikeus, who bears
your father's name, to fetch Teiresias. He'll gladly
speak to you, but me he hates for questioning
his prophetic skill.
                    And now, attendants,
bring out my arms and armor. We go now
to the ordeal of blood, and Justice who goes with us
will bring us victory. We pray to the goddess Precaution,   880
kindest of divinities, to preserve this city.

Exit ETEOKLES *to the left, followed by his attendants.* KREON
                    remains on stage throughout the Choral song.

CHORUS Ares, bringer of suffering and pain,
            why are you so possessed
        with blood and death?
            Why so out of tune
        with the feasts of Bromios,
            with the glad dances of girls,
        garlands on their heads?
            Why don't you shake
        your curls loose and sing   890
            a song to the flute's breath
        when the Graces
            lead the dance?
        Instead you incite
            Thebans and Argives
        to slaughter. You dance
            before your band of revelers
        a grim dance no music graces.
            You do not brandish
        the thyrsos in a wild whirl,   900
            you are graced

with no fawn's skin.
   But you stand in your chariot
shaking the curb-chain,
   making the colts' hoofs clatter,
and rush to the flowing Ismenos,
   where you sit with your cavalry
inspiring the Argives
   against the sons of the sown-men,
that armed, shield-bearing   910
   band of revelers
lined up along the town's stone walls
   to oppose them.
Yes, war's a terrifying god
   who has planned these horrors
for the kings of this land,
   for the Labdakids
whose life is suffering and pain.

O glen of holiest leaves,
   haunt of many wild beasts,   920
O eye of Artemis,
   snow-covered Kithairon,
you should never have nourished
   the boy abandoned to die
by exposure, the son of Jokasta,
   Oedipus, the child ejected
from the house, pierced
   with gold pins. If only
that monster of the mountain,
   the Sphinx, had not brought sorrow   930
to this city with her dissonant
   songs, she who, sent by Hades
to hurt this land once, swooping
   down on these walls, snatched up
the children of Kadmos
   with her taloned feet, high
into the untrodden light
   of the blazing upper air.

And now another ugly war
   springs from the sons 940
of Oedipus and spreads its way
   through house, through city.
What is not noble
   is never by nature good.
Nor are those children lawful—
   a mother's labor and a father's shame!
For she came to the bed
   of blood kin.
Earth, you gave birth, you gave birth once,
   so I heard in my far-away home, 950
to the race sprung from the teeth of that
   beast-eating, red-crested serpent,
glory and shame of Thebes.
   And once the gods came
to the wedding of Harmonia,
   and the walls of Thebes
rose high to the sound of the lute,
   towers rose high under the sway
of Amphion's lyre, between Dirke
   and Ismenos, two rivers whose waters 960
come pouring down to the green plain.
   And Io, our hornèd ancestor,
bore kings of the Kadmeans.
   But this city where good
was heaped on good, now stands
   above the precipice of war.

TEIRESIAS *enters from the right, one hand resting for guidance on his young daughter's shoulders.* TEIRESIAS *is blind and very old, and accordingly his movements are slow and halting. His white hair is set off by a wreath of gold leaves, and in one hand he carries a bundle of small tablets. At his side walks* MENOIKEUS, *a young man of perhaps seventeen.*

TEIRESIAS Lead on, child, like the sailor's star. You are
   the eyes for my poor blind feet. Guide my steps

toward smooth ground. Go first. Don't let your poor
weak father stumble. Your hands are young and pure.   970
Take these oracular tablets which I prepared
at the holy place where I divine the future,
observing signs and omens from the birds.
Young Menoikeus, how much farther do we have to go
to find your father? My old legs ache, and I've walked
so much I can hardly move them any more.

KREON   Courage, Teiresias. You're approaching harbor;
you're close to friends. Help hold him up, son.
Old men, like invalids, need a helping hand.

TEIRESIAS Well, we're here. Why did you send for me in such haste?   980

KREON   You'll find out. But first collect your strength
and catch your breath. Try to forget your rough journey.

TEIRESIAS I'm very tired. Only yesterday I traveled
back to Thebes from Athens. There was war there too,
against Eumolpos, and I made the Athenians victorious.
This golden crown you see on my head was awarded
to me as firstfruits from the spoils of battle.

KREON   I view that crown of yours as a good omen,
Teiresias. As you know, we're in rough water here,
waiting for the Argive wave to break.   990
King Eteokles, fully armed, has already
gone out to meet the Mycenaean attack.
He gave me orders to learn from you the knowledge
that might save the city.

TEIRESIAS If Eteokles had asked, I would have kept
my mouth shut, and withheld my oracles.
But since you ask me, I'll speak.
                                   Kreon,
this country has been diseased from the time
when Laios, disregarding the gods, fathered

wretched Oedipus, the son who married   1000
his own mother. The awful blood-stained ruin
of his sight is a shrewd contrivance of the gods,
and a warning to all Hellas. And the sons
of Oedipus who tried to hide these things
with the passage of time, as though they could
outwit the gods, acted with brutal stupidity.
They afforded their father neither honor nor exile.
They stung that anguished man to anger. Diseased,
degraded, he screamed terrible curses against them.
I warned them. I did everything I could to help—   1010
and won hatred for my pains from the sons
of Oedipus.

                              I tell you, Kreon, they both
will die, each one at the hand of his brother. Their
deaths are near. There will be corpses everywhere,
corpses piled on corpses, men struck down
by Argive and Theban arrows, and there will be mourning
and wailing in the land of Thebes.

                                                And you, too,
poor city of Thebes, will be buried with them
if no one heeds my words. Far better for Thebes
that none of the brood of Oedipus should live   1020
in this land as citizens, let alone as kings.
A father's sacred curse possesses them;
they will destroy this city.

                                        But because
the evil here outweighs the good, one way out,
one way only, remains to us. What that
way is, it is not safe for me to say.
And it will be bitter to those to whom Fate gives
the power to preserve the city.

                                        And so, farewell.
I am leaving. I am one among many. I will
suffer what happens. What else can I do?   1030

KREON (grabbing his arm) Don't go, old man!

TEIRESIAS Get your hands off me!

KREON Wait! Why are you leaving?

TEIRESIAS It is good fortune leaves you, Kreon, and not I.

KREON Tell me how to save the city and its people.

TEIRESIAS Now you want to know. Soon you will not.

KREON How can I not want to save my city?

TEIRESIAS Is that what you really want to do?
You really want to know how?

KREON What could I be more eager to know?   1040

TEIRESIAS All right, then. I'll tell you. But before I begin,
is Menoikeus still here?

KREON He's not far away. Quite near you, in fact.

TEIRESIAS Tell him to leave now, and get as far
from my prophecies as he can.

KREON My son, because he is my son, will say nothing.

TEIRESIAS Then you want me to speak with him present?

KREON He'll be happy to hear we're all going to be saved.

TEIRESIAS Then here is my prophecy. To save the city
of the Kadmeans, this is what you must do: 1050
sacrifice Menoikeus here for the good
of the land. You yourself insisted that I speak.

KREON What are you saying? What do you mean?

TEIRESIAS I have told you what you must do.

KREON You've spoken much evil in a little time.

TEIRESIAS Evil for you, but great good for the city.

KREON I wasn't listening. I didn't hear.
City, goodbye!

TEIRESIAS The man is not himself. He shies back.

KREON Goodbye, and go! I have no need of your oracle. 1060

TEIRESIAS Is your bad luck enough to kill the truth?

KREON Oh, I fall to my knees and beg you—

TEIRESIAS Why do you fall down before me?
Bow to evils that cannot be cured.

KREON Keep your mouth shut,
and don't spread this about the city.

TEIRESIAS What you command is shameful. I'll not keep quiet.

KREON What are you trying to do to me? Kill my son?

TEIRESIAS That's for others to decide. My part is to speak.

KREON How did this evil choose me and my son? 1070

TEIRESIAS You're right to challenge me and raise the question.
In the grotto where Earth brought forth the snake that
guards
Dirke's streams, Menoikeus must be sacrificed
and his red blood flow as libation for the Earth,
for the ancient guilt of Kadmos, the cause of Ares' anger,
he who now exacts vengeance for the killing
of his serpent. Do this, and Ares is your ally.
If Earth receives fruit for fruit, blood
for blood, then she who once sent up sown-men,
progeny with helmets gold as ears of wheat, 1080

will be friendly toward you. One from this race must die,
one who first saw light as a child of the serpent's teeth.
You are all that remains to us of that race of sown-men—
you and your sons. The coming marriage of Haimon
makes it unlawful to sacrifice him, for though
he is not married yet, and has not touched
the marriage bed, he has a bride. But *this* boy's life
is bound up with the city's. By dying he could
bring us safely through, and make a bitter
welcome for Adrastos and his Argives, 1090
dropping dull death over their eyes, gathering
glory for Thebes. Decide which you will save:
city or son. You've heard all I know. Child,
lead me home. Whoever practices the craft
of burnt offerings must be mad. If he reads signs
that mean misfortune for those who consult him,
he earns their scorn. And if he softens the truth
out of pity, he betrays his sacred trust. Apollo
should prophesy for men, since he alone fears no one.

Exit TEIRESIAS *to the right, led slowly by his daughter. During his exit,* MENOIKEUS *stands impassively.* KREON *is sunk in an attitude of despair.*

CHORUS
LEADER Kreon, why so silent? Why so quiet? 1100

KREON Yet this is a shock for me too.
What can anyone say? It's clear what I
should say, but I'll never sink so low that I'd
slaughter my son to ransom my city. All men
love their children, and no one would surrender
his child to be killed. I wouldn't want someone to praise
my patriotism as he was slaughtering my son.
So I myself, in the prime of life, would be
prepared to die and deliver my land. Come child,
before the whole city learns. Ignore the selfish 1110
prophecies of seers, and get away at once,

for he'll be going round the seven gates
telling all this to the captains. If you outstrip him,
you're safe. If you delay, we're lost, and you die.

MENOIKEUS Where shall I run? To what city? Which of our friends?

KREON Wherever you'll be furthest from this place.

MENOIKEUS Tell me where, I'll go.

KREON Pass by Delphi. . . .

MENOIKEUS But going where, father?

KREON Aitolia.   1120

MENOIKEUS And from there?

KREON Make for Thesprotia.

MENOIKEUS The holy temple of Dodona?

KREON Yes.

MENOIKEUS How will that help me?

KREON The god will guide you.

MENOIKEUS And what will I do for money?

KREON I'll give you gold.

MENOIKEUS Thank you, father.

KREON Now go!   1130

MENOIKEUS I'll go to Jokasta, your sister, whose breasts I sucked
when I lost my mother. When I've talked to her I'll leave,

and save my life.

KREON Yes, run! Don't hang around here!

Exit KREON *to the left.*

MENOIKEUS Women, how well I have allayed my father's fears,
          lying to get what I want! He wants me to run,
          depriving the city of its fate, and making me
          a coward. Cowardice might be forgiven an old man,
          but if I became a traitor to my country
          there'd be no pardon. No! I'll save my city.   1140
          I'll give up my soul for my country. What disgrace,
          if those who have no oracle hanging over them,
          and not in the god's power, should stand by their shields
          and fight for their land without flinching while I,
          betraying father, mother, city, run off
          like a coward. No matter where I went, I'd be
          contemptible. No, I swear by Zeus who lives
          among the stars, and by blood-red Ares who once
          made the sown men who sprang from the soil lords
          of this land, that I will take my stand on a high   1150
          battlement, and sacrifice myself
          in the serpent's sacred dark enclosure, where
          the prophet said that I should free my land.

Exit MENOIKEUS *to the right.*

CHORUS You came, you came,
            wingèd child of earth,
        of Ekhidna who lives underground,
            snatcher of men, killer of men,
        maker of groans, greedy
            mongrel monster
        with wandering wings   1160
            and claws sticky
        with raw meat.
            You who grabbed boys

from Dirke's banks and
    with your riddling dirge
brought a murderous Fury
    and bloody anguish
against this land.
    A blood-boltered god
sent you to make   1170
    mothers mourn
and young girls cry
    in their chambers.
Groans echo through the streets,
    gusts of sighs and wailing
wherever the wingèd woman
    snatched some man
from the city.

As time passed,
    Apollo's priestess sent   1180
pitiful Oedipus to this land
    of Thebes, first
to the people's joy,
    then to their sorrow.
For he made an evil marriage
    with his mother
when he'd unraveled the riddle
    and so stained our city,
wading through blood
    into polluted strife,   1190
and casting down his children
    with his curses—
the miserable man!
    We admire, we admire
the young man who goes
    to his death to defend
this land, leaving
    Kreon, but bringing
victory to the seven-towered
    gates of this city.   1200

May we mother such a child!
  May we bear such sons,
O Pallas, you who held
  the stone that slew
the serpent, you who turned
  the mind of Kadmos
to the deed from which
  all this devouring
and destruction is derived!

MESSENGER *rushes in from the left and pounds on the palace
doors.*

MESSENGER Is anyone inside there? Open up!   1210
  I must see Jokasta.

(pause)

Inside there! You're taking your time, Queen Jokasta,
come out to hear what I have to say.
Wipe your eyes. Stop your groans.

Enter JOKASTA *from the palace.*

JOKASTA Dear friend, you haven't brought the news of Eteokles'
  death, have you? The death of the man by whose shield
  you've always marched, warding off every attack.
  Is my son alive or dead? I must know.

MESSENGER Don't tremble so. He's alive. I can quiet your fears.

JOKASTA The circuit of walls, with their seven towers, they're safe?   1220

MESSENGER Nothing is changed. The city isn't sacked.

JOKASTA How close did the Argives come?

MESSENGER Too close. But Kadmean courage was stronger
  than the spears of Mycenae.

JOKASTA Answer me one thing, and swear by the gods
your answer's true. Is Polyneikes still alive?

MESSENGER Both your sons are still alive.

JOKASTA Bless you! Now tell me, how did you turn back
the Argive army from the gates when you were
cooped up in the towers? Tell me, so I may go   1230
to the blind old man inside the house here
and bring him joy, since this land's been saved.

MESSENGER When Kreon's son had killed himself for his country
by standing on the high tower and piercing his neck
with his sword, this land's savior, your son
placed seven companies and captains at
the seven gates, to guard against the Argive army,
ordering reserves of horsemen and hoplites
to their stations as the second line of defense
at the wall's weak points. From the sheer citadel   1240
he watched the white Argive shields swarm down
the hill of Teumessos, and, approaching the earthworks,
break into a run and close in on the city.
Battlecry and trumpet broke out together,
from our walls and from over there. Then
Parthenopaios, son of Atalanta
who hunts with hounds, was first to lead a company
with shields pressed rim to rim against the Neitian gate.
At the center of his shield was the emblem of his house,
Atalanta shooting the Aitolian boar. The seer   1250
Amphiaraos attacked the Protidan gate,
with sacrificial victims in his chariot,
but wisely bearing no proud blazons on his weapons.
Hippomedon strode to the Ogygian gate
with a sign at the center of his shield. The sign
was Argos, eyes spangling his whole body.
Some eyes were open, watching their stars rise,
while some were closed since other stars had set.
All this we could see clearly when he was dead.

Tydeus took his place before the Homoloidan gate.   1260
On his shield he had a lion's pelt
with bristling mane, and Prometheus the Titan
carrying a torch to burn the city. At the Krenaian gate
the attack was started by your son Polyneikes.
On his shield the fillies of Potniai leapt
and fled in panic—they were somehow made to move
on pivots from inside, and spun round so
thcy really scemed to rage. But Kapaneus,
angry as Ares in battlc, lcd his company
against the Elektran gate. On his iron-backed shield   1270
an earthborn giant carried on his shoulders
the whole city which he had wrenched from its roots
with crowbars—a hint to us what our city
would suffer. Adrastos was at the seventh gate,
his shield filled with a hundred hydra heads,
the glory of the Argives. And from our walls
they grabbed the Kadmean children in their jaws.
I had time to note all this as I was carrying
the password to our commanders. Then we began
to press the attack with javelins and arrows,   1280
with slingshots, and a clatter of stones. When we
were winning, Tydeus and Polyneikes both
shouted at the same time: "Descendants of Danaos,
you hoplites, you cavalry and charioteers,
why hang back and wait for their projectiles
to smash you to bits? Why don't you charge in a body
at the gates?" When they heard this, no one
held back, and many fell, heads laid open.
And you would have seen throngs of our soldiers tumbling
and diving to the soil, lifeless, soaking   1290
parched earth with gouts of blood. And now
the Arcadian, Atalanta's son, crashing into
the gate like a whirlwind, calls for twin-blade axes,
and torches to raze the town to the ground. But
Periklymenos, son of the sea-god, stopped
his raving with a stone, a coping-stone
from the battlements, heavy as a cartload.

He crushed the blond head and shattered the sutures
of his skull, and the cheeks, already red-bearded,
turned red with blood. Only a lifeless body   1300
will go home to his mother, she of the deft bow,
daughter of Mount Mainalos. When he saw
this gate was safe, Eteokles went to the others,
and I went with him. I saw Tydeus with
his shieldbearers tight about him hurling their
Aitolian spears at the towers, so the defenders left
their clifflike battlements. But back again
came your son, like a hunter summoning his pack.
He regrouped and rallied his men and set them again
on the towers. We took off to another gate since we   1310
had saved this one from falling.

                             But how can I
describe how Kapaneus raged? Holding
a long-necked ladder, he came running, boasting
not even one of Zeus' thunderbolts could stop him
from taking the city apart from top to bottom.
While he spoke he was being stoned, so
crawling up the ladder, rung by rung,
he crouched under his shield. But just as he
was climbing over the coping of the walls,
Zeus struck him with lightning. The earth rang,   1320
terrifying everyone. Kapeneus' limbs
were split apart, scattered everywhere.
His hair sailed into the sky, his blood spurted
onto the earth, his arms and legs whirled
about like Ixion's on his wheel. His charred body
crashed to the ground. When Adrastos realized Zeus
was against him, he drew back his men beyond
the ditch. Our men too saw the favorable sign
from Zeus, and charged out—chariots, cavalry,
hoplites—and began thrusting their spears right into   1330
the heart of the Argive line. It was pandemonium.
Many lost their lives—they fell from their chariot-rails,
wheels shot into the air, axle heaped on axle,
corpse piled on corpse.

                        Well, today we've stopped

the destruction of our towers. If this town
will be as fortunate in future, that's up to the gods.
For now, one of the gods has saved her.

CHORUS Victory's a glorious thing, and if
LEADER the gods grant even better fortune
may I share it.   1340

JOKASTA Fortune and the gods have been good, for my
sons live, and this land too is spared.
But Kreon's reaped the harvest of this marriage
I made with Oedipus. He's lost his son—
which benefits the city, but brings him only grief.
Get back to your report. What else are my sons planning?

MESSENGER Forget the future. So far you've enjoyed good fortune.

JOKASTA That sounds suspicious. I can't let it pass.

MESSENGER What is there to say? Your sons are safe.

JOKASTA I want to know if all will continue to be well.   1350

MESSENGER Let me go. Your son can't spare his servant.

JOKASTA You're hiding something dreadful in the dark.

MESSENGER I won't bring bad news hot after good.

JOKASTA You must, unless you can vanish into air.

MESSENGER Why wouldn't you let me go, after the good news,
instead of insisting I reveal the bad?
Your sons—with more swagger than sense—intend
to fight hand to hand in front of the armies.
To the assembled Argives and Kadmeans
they have spoken words that should never have been spoken.   1360
Eteokles started it, standing on
a high tower, insisting on silence in

65

the armies: "Commanders of the Danaans here
assembled, citizens of Thebes: do not
for my sake or the sake of Polyneikes
gamble away your souls. I all alone,
to save you from harm, will fight with my brother,
and if I kill him, I'll rule my kingdom alone.
But if he worsts me, this land is all his."
That is what he said, and your son Polyneikes   1370
rushed from the ranks at once to second his words,
while both Argives and Thebans shouted their approval.
On these terms a truce was made, and in
the no man's land between the armies, the leaders
took oaths to abide by it. So these young men,
both sons of Oedipus, sheathed their bodies
in bronze, and their comrades helped each arm.
They stood gleaming in the sun; their faces
did not pale. Each was hot and eager
to hurl his spear at the other. From all sides   1380
their comrades encouraged them with words like:
"Polyneikes, you can set up a statue to Zeus
as trophy, and bring glory to Argos." Or:
"Eteokles, now your city is at stake.
If you win, you will be king." This is how
they incited them to fight. Then the priests
sacrificed sheep to see whether the victims
burned with stiff spires of flame, or whether the fires
flickered damply. They marked the highest mounting
of the blaze, which signals victory, or loss.   1390
But if, with wise words, spells, or potions, you
can help—go stop your sons from this disastrous
fight. There's terrible danger.

JOKASTA Antigone, my child, come out here in front of the house.
The gods have decreed you should take no more pleasure
in dances, or other girlish delights. Instead, you and I
must stop your brothers from dying at each other's hands.

                        Enter ANTIGONE *from the palace.*

ANTIGONE Mother, what new calamity have you
                called me out to hear?

JOKASTA Daughter, your brothers' lives are lost.   1400

ANTIGONE What are you saying?

JOKASTA They have decided to fight hand to hand.

ANTIGONE What are you trying to tell me, mother?

JOKASTA Nothing that will please you. Now come with me.

ANTIGONE And leave here? Where are you taking me?

JOKASTA To the army.

ANTIGONE I feel awkward among crowds.

JOKASTA This is no time for modesty.

ANTIGONE Then what will I do?

JOKASTA Bring an end to your brothers' feuding.   1410

ANTIGONE How, mother?

JOKASTA We'll bend our knees, and beg them.
               (*to* MESSENGER) Lead us to that no man's land!
               (*to* ANTIGONE) Quick, quick, girl! If I can reach my sons
               before they fight, my life is saved.
               If they die, I'll die with them.

               Exeunt JOKASTA *and* ANTIGONE *in haste, led by the*
                                     MESSENGER

CHORUS Aiai, aiai,
             My heart shivers
             with a sudden pang.
               Through my body   1420

pity flows,
    pity for the poor mother.
Two sons. . . . Which
    will pierce—oh,
her suffering—
    his brother's neck,
which will pierce
    his brother's soul
with bloody stroke
    through the shield?   1430
And I, miserable creature,
    which dead man shall I mourn?
Oh god, oh god,
    twin beasts, blood-crazed souls,
brandishing spears
    to cut a fallen foe
to pieces. Fools,
    ever to think
of single combat!
    With Asiatic laments   1440
I will raise a cry of mourning,
    and give the dead
the tribute of my tears.
    Fated death is not far off.
Daylight will decide
    what is to be.
This death need not have happened,
    but the Erinyes ordained it.

There, I see Kreon walking this way.
His face is clouded.   1450
I will stop this mourning.

Enter KREON *from the right, walking slowly and with bowed*
                                                        head.

KREON   What can I do now? Shall I start crying
        and feel sorry for myself, or for my city
        swathed in fogs as if floating over Acheron?

My son lies lifeless, having given his life
for this land. For this he gained a noble name,
but a name that crazes me with grief. I have
just taken his body from the serpent's lair—my whole
house cries out in anguish. Now I have come,
this old man's come, to his old sister Jokasta   1460
so she may wash the wreckage that was my son,
and lay it out. He who has not yet died
ought to honor the gods below by honoring the dead.

CHORUS   Kreon, your sister's left the house, and taken
LEADER   young Antigone with her.

KREON   Where have they gone? What new crisis now?

CHORUS   She heard her sons have challenged each other to fight
LEADER   in single combat for the kingdom.

KREON   What? I was so engrossed in tending
my son's corpse I've heard nothing of all this.   1470

CHORUS   Kreon, your sister set off some time back.
LEADER   The fight to the death must be over by now:
The sons of Oedipus must have settled their score.

                    Enter MESSENGER *from the left.*

MESSENGER   Miserable as I am, what can I say?

KREON   This prelude means that we are lost.

MESSENGER   I bring terrible news.

KREON   To add to what we have already. Out with it!

MESSENGER   Your sister's sons are dead.

KREON   Grief, grief for us all.
House of Oedipus, have you heard,   1480
two sons killed by the same calamity?

69

CHORUS
LEADER   It would weep if it had feelings.

KREON   I am crushed by this weight of misfortunes.

MESSENGER   There is more.

KREON   What else could there be?

MESSENGER   Your sister died with her sons.

CHORUS   The lament, raise it,
      the cries!
    With your white arms
      rain blows   1490
    on your head!

KREON   Miserable Jokasta, what a close
    to your marriage and your life the Sphinx's
    riddle has made! How did it happen, this triple death?

MESSENGER   You know of our success at the towers. You could see
    it all from the walls. Then when the young sons of Oedipus
    had put on their bronze armor, they came and stood
    between the armies, two brothers, two commanders,
    bent on combat. With a look toward Argos, Polyneikes
    began his prayer: "Lady Hera, I am yours since I married   1500
    the daughter of Adrastos, and I live in your land.
    Let me kill my brother, and steep my right hand,
    bringer of success, in his blood." He prayed
    for a crown of shame, to kill his brother. Many
    were overcome by tears at this terrible thing.
    They looked at each other, exchanging glances.
    But Eteokles, facing the temple of gold-shielded
    Athena, prayed: "Pure daughter of Zeus, let me
    plunge this sword into my brother's side,
    and kill the man who comes to plunder my land."   1510
    But when the firebrand was flung—a sign,

like the Etruscan trumpet, for the battle
to begin—they charged, and like wild boars slashing
with their tusks, they slashed at each other, cheeks
flecked with slaver. Then they rushed in with spears,
and crouched beneath the circle of their shields
so steel might glance harmlessly off. If one saw
the other's eye over the rim he jabbed
his spear at him, trying to get him first.
But they kept their eyes so sharp at slits in the shield,   1520
thrusts were spent without effect. More sweat
trickled down spectators than fighters, their friends
were so afraid. But Eteokles stumbled against
a stone, and put a limb outside the shield.
Polyneikes, seeing an opening for
his steel, struck it with his spear: the Argive
shaft pierced Eteokles' thigh. The whole
Argive army raised a warcry. But,
seeing the shoulder that had dealt the blow
exposed, the injured Eteokles stabbed   1530
Polyneikes in the chest, which cheered
the Kadmeans. But the spearhead broke off.
Desperate, Polyneikes retreated
step by step. Then, seizing a lump of marble,
he threw it, and snapped his brother's spear
in half. So the battle stood balanced since both
had lost their spears. Then, seizing their sword-hilts,
they strode to the same spot. Their shields clashed:
locked together, they raised the clamor of combat,
till Eteokles thought of a Thessalian feint   1540
he'd learned when he visited their land. Abandoning
his attack, he brought his left foot back
behind the shield and, careful to protect
his belly, put his right leg out and plunged
his sword through Polyneikes' navel,
driving it clean to the backbone. Bending
double, so ribs and bowels meet, Polyneikes
drops with a gush of blood. Eteokles,
now in full command, throwing down his sword,

begins to strip his brother's armor off,   1550
and, being so intent on that, ignored
all else. And that was his ruin. For Polyneikes,
gasping for breath, but still clutching his sword,
just manages to thrust it out and lodge it
in Eteokles' liver, Polyneikes, the first
to fall. So, gripping earth with their teeth,
the two now lie side by side.
They do not share the kingdom.

CHORUS Oh, Oedipus, how I mourn your sorrows.
LEADER A god seems to have heard your curses.   1560

MESSENGER There are still more sorrows.
When her sons had fallen and were leaving this life,
at that moment, their mother, with Antigone,
arrived breathless and rushed to them. Seeing them
breathing their last, she moaned: "O sons, I came
quickly to your cries, but too late!" Dropping
down beside them, she began to weep and mourn,
grieving that her breasts had ever given milk.
Their sister, her companion in grief,
cried out: "Our mother's comfort in old age,   1570
destroyers of my marriage, my dearest brothers!"—
But then Jokasta heaved a heavy sigh.
Eteokles heard his mother. Holding out
a dank hand, he did not speak, yet spoke
to her with tears from his eyes, token of his love.
But his brother still breathed. Staring at
his sister and old mother, Polyneikes said:
"We are dead, mother. I pity you and this
my sister here, and that corpse, my brother.
He who was closest to me became my enemy,   1580
Though love still bound us. Take me, you who brought me
into this world, and you born of the same mother,
bring me to the soil of my fathers, and soothe
the angry city so I may get just as much
of my father's land as I need, even if all else

is lost." He put his hand upon his eyes
himself, and "Goodbye," he said, "for now the dark
is closing in on me." Both breathed out
their bitter lives together. But the mother,
seeing this sight of misery, overcome with suffering,   1590
seized a sword from the dead and did a dreadful thing.
Through the center of her throat she stuck the steel,
and now she lies in death between her sons,
embracing both.
                The soldiers sprang to their feet
and started to quarrel. Our side claimed my master
won, theirs that Eteokles was the winner.
The generals argued too. Some said Polyneikes
struck first, others replied that since both died
victory meant nothing. At this point, Antigone withdrew
and the soldiers rushed to arms. By happy foresight,   1600
the Thebans were sitting by their weapons, so we attacked
before the Argives had time to buckle on their armor.
Not one stood his ground. The plain swarmed with their flight
and flowed with the blood of bodies pierced by our lances.
When we had won, some set up a statue of Zeus
as a trophy, while others stripped shields and weapons
from Argive corpses and sent the spoils to the city.
Still others are with Antigone, bearing bodies here
for loved ones to lament. Some of this day's struggles
ended in joy for our city, others in bitter sorrow.   1610

CHORUS These sorrows are not
      just a tale that's told.
Soon you can see
      at the palace door
three corpses dropped by fate
      into common death,
winning dark eternity
      together.

Enter ANTIGONE *from the left, followed by soldiers who carry
the corpses of* JOKASTA, ETEOKLES, *and* POLYNEIKES. *While*

ANTIGONE *sings and dances her dirge, the soldiers slowly and*
reverentially carry the bodies to the center of the stage, set
them down before the palace, and form a guard of honor
beside them. KREON *remains motionless on the right, ab-*
sorbed in his grief.

ANTIGONE Not veiling the silk
    of the cheek   1620
where my curls fall,
    and not feeling
a young girl's shame
    at the blood-red flush
under my eyes
    or the blush
on my face,
    I am borne along,
a bacchante of the dead.
    I tear off the band   1630
that bound my hair.
    I drop the softness
of this saffron robe.
    I conduct the corpses
with my many groans.
    Polyneikes, you lived up
to your quarrelsome name—
    to my city's sorrow!
Your quarrel (not quarrel
    but killing on killing!)   1640
has soaked the house
    of Oedipus in blood,
bitter blood.
    House, what choral song
or music of lament
    to my tears, to
my tears, can I
    summon?
I bring these three bodies,
    mother and sons,   1650

the delights of the Fury
   who destroyed the house
of Oedipus
   from the moment that he grasped
the monster's song,
   so hard to grasp,
and killed her while she sang.
   O my father, my father,
out of all the many sufferings
   this flesh of a day 1660
is heir to, what Greek
   or barbarian, what
famous prince from the past
   has suffered
such raw sorrow?
   O creature that I am,
how I cry out!
   What bird, perched
on the high-crowned branch
   of olive or oak, 1670
with the tears of a mother bereft
   echoes my groans?
With tear upon tear
   I drone this dirge,
alone,
   about to lead my life
to the end of my days
   among my tears.
On whose tomb shall I toss
   the offering shorn 1680
from my hair?
   On the breasts of the woman
who nursed me,
   or the wounds
cut into my brothers'
   corpses?
Ay, ay!
   Leave your house, old father.

Show your blind eyes,
   your pitiful age,   1690
you who at home,
   having drawn down
dark mist over your eyes,
   drag out a long life.
Do you hear me as you drift
   on aged feet
through dark halls
   or lie in misery
on your bed?

The palace doors open. OEDIPUS *emerges alone, tapping his*
way with a stick.

OEDIPUS Girl, why do you goad me into the light   1700
   with your terrible tears, a bedridden creature
   from dark chambers, this stick support for my
   blind foot? A shadow of thin air,
   a corpse from the clay,
   a wingèd dream?

ANTIGONE Father, you must know this disastrous news:
   your sons are dead. And so is your wife.

OEDIPUS Ah, my suffering . . . I groan for all this,
   I cry out.
   How did three souls leave the light at once?   1710
   What death did they die? Speak, child!

ANTIGONE I don't say this to reproach or mock you, but in misery
   I say your avenging spirit, laden with sword
   and fire and ghastly battles, has gone against
   your sons—oh, my father!

OEDIPUS Oh, oh. . . .

ANTIGONE Why these groans now?

76

OEDIPUS They were still my children. . . .

ANTIGONE You would endure agony in those sockets
            that once were eyes if you could still see   1720
            the sun's chariot sweep across the sky,
            and see the bodies of the dead.

OEDIPUS My sons' fate is clear. But my wife, my poor wife,
            what death swept her away, child?

ANTIGONE Everyone heard her tears and cries.
            She offered her breast to her sons;
            a suppliant, she rushed
            to offer it in supplication.
            She saw her sons at the Elektran gate
            where they lunged at each other with spears   1730
            in a field flowering with lotus.
            The mother saw them, lions
            in their lairs, warlike still
            despite their wounds, and the
            crimson libation
            of cold blood
            which Ares offers
            and Hades accepts.
            Seizing the hammered bronze sword
            from the slain   1740
            she dipped it in her flesh.
            Gripped by grief for her sons
            she fell on top
            of their bodies.
            The god who brings all things to pass
            has heaped on our house
            all this suffering.

CHORUS This day has let loose much evil
LEADER upon the house of Oedipus.

KREON An end to these tears! It's time to think of burials   1750

and tombs. Oedipus, listen. Power over
this land was placed in my hands by your son
Eteokles, when he gave the hand of Antigone
your daughter to Haimon with a dowry.
I forbid you, therefore, to live longer in this land,
for Teiresias declared clearly that so long
as you linger here, Thebes will never flourish.
So leave us. I do not speak in arrogance,
nor as your foe, but because I fear your avenging
spirit could hurt this land.   1760

OEDIPUS From my birth I was fated to be wretched
and miserable, more than any other man.
Even unborn, even before I came
into the light from my mother's womb,
Apollo warned Laios I would become my own
father's killer. What a creature I am!
And when I was born, the father who made me
tried to kill me, thinking he'd made a natural
antagonist, since he was fated to die
at my hands. And he sent me, still puling   1770
for the breast, to be food for beasts. But I
was kept alive—Kithairon ought to have dropped
into the depthless chasms of Tartaros since
it didn't destroy me! But no, the god granted me
to serve Polybos, my master. And when
I had cut down my own father, quarry of demons
that I am, I bedded my mother, and begot
the brothers and sons that I have slain. So
I conveyed Laios' curse. But I wasn't born
so bereft of sense that in these acts   1780
against my sons and my own eyes I cannot
see the gods' intervention.
                                        Well then, what
must this miserable man do? Who will come
with me to guide my blind steps? She who has died?
If she were living she would. Or my fine brace
of sons? They're far from me. Or am I still

so young that I can make a living for myself?
Where? Why are you killing me, Kreon? For you
do kill me, if you cast me out of this land.
Well, I'll not be abject and twine my arms   1790
around your knees. I won't betray my nobility
of birth, even if it goes the worse for me.

KREON   I'm glad you've said you will not shame my knees.
I cannot let you live here. As for these corpses,
this one must be carried into the house.
The other, who came to sack this city, his home,
this Polyneikes, dump him with the others
outside the borders of this land.
                                        Now proclaim this
to the Kadmeans. Anyone who is caught crowning
this corpse with wreaths of green parsley, or placing it   1800
in the earth, will earn death for his pains.
As for you, Antigone, get inside the house,
and behave as befits a pure and virgin girl
whom dawning day will bring to Haimon's bed.

ANTIGONE   O father, we sorrowing creatures lie steeped in evils.
I moan more for you than for the dead.
It's not that your life's divided into dark
and light: you've walked in darkness from birth.
                                        But you,
our renowned new ruler, why do you want to insult
my father by shoving him out of the country? And why   1810
make laws against a miserable corpse?

KREON   Eteokles decided that, not I.

ANTIGONE   A foolish decision. And you're a fool to obey.

KREON   What do you mean? Isn't it right to carry out commands?

ANTIGONE   Not if they're vicious, spat out with venom.

KREON Isn't it right to give this body to dogs?

ANTIGONE No! For the "right" you impose on him is not just.

KREON He came as a stranger to destroy his own city.

ANTIGONE And for that he paid his penalty to the gods.

KREON Let him pay the penalty also with his tomb.   1820

ANTIGONE How was he wrong? He only came for his share in the land.

KREON Once more, just so you can grasp it: this man will go
    unburied.

ANTIGONE *I* will bury him, even if the city forbid it.

KREON Then you bury yourself too, close by his corpse.

ANTIGONE Is it not noble for two friends to lie together?

KREON Grab her, and get her into the house!

                    ANTIGONE *throws herself on* POLYNEIKES' *corpse.*

ANTIGONE I will not let go of this corpse!

KREON Young woman, the gods' decrees go counter to your wishes.

ANTIGONE This too has been decreed: offer the dead no outrage.

KREON I tell you, no one shall pile the damp dust around him.   1830

ANTIGONE Kreon, I beg you, by his mother Jokasta here . . .

KREON You're wasting your time. Nothing can change my mind.

ANTIGONE At least let me bathe the body.

KREON That too the city forbids.

ANTIGONE But—to cover his cruel wounds with bandages . . .

KREON In no way will you reverence this corpse.

ANTIGONE My precious brother! At least I'll press your mouth to mine.

KREON It bodes no good, this wailing before your wedding.

ANTIGONE You're mad! I marry your son? Not while there's breath in
      my body!

KREON You have no alternative. How will you avoid the marriage?   1840

ANTIGONE This night will number me among the daughters of Danaos.

KREON You see how openly she insults us?

ANTIGONE This steel knows what I'll do, this sword by which I swear.

KREON Why so fierce to be free of this wedding?

ANTIGONE With this most unfortunate of fathers I'll face exile.

KREON There's nobility in you—and no small amount of nonsense.

ANTIGONE No doubt. But I'll die with him. Maybe that will open
      your eyes.

KREON Then clear out! You'll not kill my son. Leave at once!

    KREON *signals the soldiers to follow, and exits to the right.*

OEDIPUS O daughter, it's kind of you to care for me this way . . .

ANTIGONE How would I feel if I married, and you wandered into
      exile alone?   1850

OEDIPUS Stay here and be happy. I shall accept my lot.

ANTIGONE And who will be your guide, blind as you are.

OEDIPUS Falling where fate guided, I shall lie on the ground.

ANTIGONE Now where is the Oedipus of the glorious riddle?

OEDIPUS Gone. The same day blessed and broke me.

ANTIGONE Then shouldn't I too share your pain?

OEDIPUS It's a hard life for a girl exiled with her blind father.

ANTIGONE No, but noble, if the mind is noble.

OEDIPUS Then lead me on, so I may touch your mother.

ANTIGONE Here, put your hand on your dead wife.   1860

OEDIPUS My mother, my most miserable wife.

ANTIGONE All evils lie heaped with her here.

OEDIPUS The bodies of Eteokles and Polyneikes, where are they lying?

ANTIGONE Stretched out in front of you, father, side by side.

OEDIPUS Place my blind hand on their unlucky faces.

ANTIGONE Here, hold your dead sons with your hand.

OEDIPUS Dear fallen sons, wretches fathered by a wretch.

ANTIGONE The name "Polyneikes" is dearest to me.

OEDIPUS Even now, child, Apollo's oracle is being fulfilled.

ANTIGONE In what way? Do you mean there's worse to come?   1870

OEDIPUS I am to die an exile in Athens.

ANTIGONE Where? What Attic refuge will receive you?

OEDIPUS Holy Kolonos, home of the horse god.
But come. Help this blind father of yours,
since you wish to share in his flight.
To exile.

ANTIGONE Stretch here your dear hand,
old father.
I am your guide,
the breeze to blow your ship.   1880

OEDIPUS I am on my way, child.
Be my sad guide.

ANTIGONE Yes, yes, saddest
of the girls of Thebes.

OEDIPUS Where shall I put my foot?
So. Come, be my staff.

ANTIGONE This way. Come with me. This way.
Walk this way
with all the strength of a dream.

OEDIPUS That it should come to this, wandering,   1890
an old man, having to flee my own country.
I am suffering, suffering.

ANTIGONE Suffering? Why speak of it? The god
of retribution doesn't even see evil,
let alone punish mad deeds.

OEDIPUS I am he who climbed the height of wisdom,
the man who unraveled the beast-woman's dark riddle.

ANTIGONE Why hark back to the Sphinx's bitter days?
             Speak no more of past successes.
             All the time, this was in store—   1900
             exile from your land and death somewhere.

OEDIPUS O people of a famous land, look
             at Oedipus. I alone battered to bits
             the power of the bloodthirsty Sphinx. And now
             I am driven dishonored, in torment, from this city.
             But why these tears, why all this useless whining?
             I am only a man, and must bear what the gods give.

        OEDIPUS, *supported by* ANTIGONE, *slowly moves off to the
                       left; the* CHORUS *exit to the right.*

NOTES AND GLOSSARY

NOTES

1-233 Prologue

1 *Sun, flaring in your flames* The play begins in our manuscripts with two verses whose authenticity is highly suspect: "O you cutting a path through heaven among the stars, and mounted on a chariot inlaid with gold, . . ." M. W. Haslam, "Euripides, *Phoenissae* 1-2 and Sophocles, *Electra* 1" *Greek, Roman, and Byzantine Studies* 16 (1975), 149-74, shows that an early collection of hypotheses to Euripidean plays cites our line 1 as the first line of the *Phoenician Women*.

4 *Here he married Harmonia* The genealogy of the Theban royal house as it appears in the *Phoenician Women*:

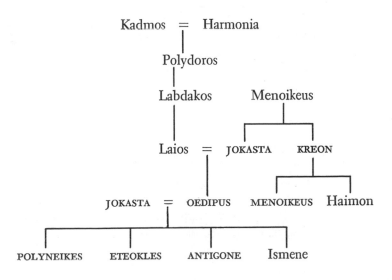

6 *Menoikeus' child*   The manuscripts insert a line at this point, "And my brother Kreon was born of one and the same mother." Jokasta's relation to Kreon is duly mentioned in line 41; whoever introduced it at this point presumably wished to emphasize it.

45f. *the scepter of this country*   In the manuscripts, this is preceded by a line of similar import: "And so he was set up as ruler of this land." One or the other of these lines is likely to be an interpolated doublet, and possibly both are spurious.

115 *made with music*   The Greek text speaks merely of "stony work consisting of a wall," but the word translated as "work" (*organon*) is often used to mean "musical instrument," and Amphion raised the walls of Thebes by playing his lyre (cf. line 956ff.).

151 *I saw on their shields*   In the manuscripts, this is followed by two probably spurious verses: "when I went to make a truce with your brother [= line 93f.]; and having seen the signs, I know the men in their armor" (a clumsy expansion of the idea in 151).

222 *Amymone*   Poseidon rescued this daughter of Danaos from the advances of a satyr when she was fetching water for her father, and then seduced her himself. To commemorate the affair, he struck a rock at Lerna with his trident and produced an ever-flowing spring.

234-304 *Parodos* or choral entrance-song: The Chorus enter in three rows of five, led by a flute player. Their song identifies them and explains their presence in Thebes, but the central part is devoted to their final destination, Delphi, the pan-Hellenic shrine shared by Apollo and Dionysos. These gods are not invoked in Nietzschean contrast, but as harmonious emblems of peace and civilization in contrast to the destructive power of Ares (war) that hangs over Thebes.

236 *from the island of Phoenicia*   The ancient city of Tyre was built on an island, but because of supposed difficulties in the chorus' description of their voyage, some scholars have preferred to take the phrase as referring to Carthage, a Tyrian colony. It is difficult to see how the audience could have understood so imprecise an allusion. As for the voyage, one can easily enough imagine the maidens sailing south of Crete, west of the Peloponnese (the Ionian sea refers broadly to the waters between Greece and Italy, and puts us in mind of Io, ancestor of

Phoenicians and Thebans alike), and through the gulf of Korinth to the port of Thebes. From Thebes they were to have been taken to their final destination, Apollo's sanctuary at Delphi, but the outbreak of war has intervened.

254ff. *the towers of Laios that are / kin to the glorious line / of Agenor* Behind this bold figure is a claim of kinship between Tyrians and Thebans: Agenor was the father both of Phoinix, ancestor of the Phoninikians, and Kadmos, founder of Thebes. At 289ff., the Chorus take the claim of common ancestry even further back, to the Argive priestess Io, Agenor's great-grandmother on most accounts.

264ff. *O rock, / flashing with the flare / of tossing torches* Reference is to the lower slopes of Mount Parnassos, which rise directly behind the sanctuary at Delphi, where at certain times strange shimmering lights could be seen. These were explained as the god and his revelers dancing with torches in their hands.

268f. *you vine that daily / let drop* A miraculous vine in the precinct of Dionysos at Delphi was said to produce one ripe cluster of grapes each day for the god's libation.

272f. *cave of the serpent / Apollo slew* Apollo, while still a child slew the monstrous Pytho in order to claim Delphi for his own seat. Cf. Kadmos' slaying of the chthonian serpent at Thebes (lines 759ff.).

291 *horn-bearing Io* Zeus changed Io to a cow in order to conceal her from his jealous consort, Hera.

300 *O Pelasgian Argos* The Pelasgians were, for the Greeks, the old autochthonous inhabitants of their land. Argos appears with this epithet as early as Homer (*Iliad* 2.681), and Aeschylus, in the *Suppliants*, makes the eponymous Pelasgos king of Argos and most of mainland Greece.

305-727 *First episode*

387 *his share in the solemnities* The Theban river is depicted as a kinsman to whom would befall the task of providing water for the ritual ablution of bride and bridegroom on the day before the wedding. He is denied his privilege because the wedding was held elsewhere. Likewise, the arrival of the bride is called silent in line 391 by contrast to the celebration that should have greeted her, had she really come to Thebes.

415 *hatred within families* In the manuscripts, this is followed by four lines that appear to be an awkward attempt at pathos: "How enmity finds reconciliation difficult. Well, what is my old father doing within the house, whose sight is dark? And my two sisters? Could it be that they lament my miserable exile?" The problem here is not primarily linguistic— the first questions are not, as has been suggested, bad Greek for "how are they faring?" but quite standard Greek for "what are they doing?" to which the last question implies a possible answer. But the whole passage is intrusive and receives no reply whatever from Jokasta.

483 *It may be trite* The closing lines of Polyneikes' speech look suspiciously like the sententious addition of a later interpolator, inspired perhaps by Polyneikes' complaints of poverty at 441. The arguments for deletion are not conclusive, however, and we have decided to retain the lines despite our doubts. (Certainly, both the jarring sentiment and the anti-climactic ending can be paralleled elsewhere in Euripides.)

605f. *For the wise man sufficient / is enough* The manuscripts add four lines at this point: "Mortals do not possess goods as their own; rather we hold and care for what belongs to the gods. Whenever they wish, they take it back again. Wealth is not steadfast, but merely of a day." We are persuaded by the argument that these lines are Euripidean, but interpolated from another context by a process of transfer from the margin of a copy-text into the body of the play.

666 *gods of the white horses* These are Amphion and Zethos, whom Euripides here and elsewhere depicts as Dioskouroi, divine offspring of Zeus like the Spartan twins Kastor and Polydeukes.

717f. *Apollo, lord / of the roadways* Polyneikes addresses the cult image of Apollo Agyieus that stood outside the doorway of Greek dwellings, great and small, to propitiate both arrivals and departures; it thus makes a natural starting-point for the farewell to his house and familiar surroundings. The cult image was usually a plain conical pillar of stone.

728-796 First *stasimon*

778 *Epaphos* is an appropriate recipient of the Chorus's prayers as ancestor of both Thebans and Phoenicians; he was grandfather of Agenor (see note on 254ff.).

787 *Persephone and dear Demeter* The cult of these goddesses was apparently prominent in Thebes; the scholiast records a story that Zeus gave Thebes to Persephone as a wedding present. This passage, however, appears to reflect the Athenian traditions as much as Theban: the torches held by the goddesses (793f.) reflect the importance of fire in the Eleusinian mysteries. In any case, invoking the goddesses reinforces the ode's themes of the soil and its fertility.

797-881 *Second episode*

877 *with his prophetic skill* This is followed in the manuscripts by five suspiciously clumsy lines: "To the city and to you, Kreon, I command this: if I should win, never to entomb the corpse of Polyneikes in this Theban earth, but to kill the one who buries him, even if it is a dear one. So much for you. But to my attendants I say," etc. The arguments for deletion are complex, and perhaps not perfectly decisive, but we have found them persuasive. Apart from linguistic arguments, two general points can be made. 1. The lines embody an almost coy foreshadowing of what is to come in the legendary tradition. For example, if Eteokles wins, he can see to preventing his brother's burial, except in the unlikely (but, as we know, true) case that he should both win and be killed. And the clause "even if it is a dear one," seeming all too neatly tailored to the case of Antigone. 2. Eteokles has announced the "one thing" (873) that still remains to be done. Now he is ready to arm and depart. The lines are intrusive.

882-966 *Second stasimon* The first part develops a consistent metaphoric depiction of Ares, god of war, as a kind of perverse incarnation of the Theban god Dionysos, lord of wine, music and revelry. Rather than joining in the festive dance (885-93), Ares is dancing-master of death, shaking curb-chains instead of the thyrsus, and inspiring his devotees to slaughter.

917f. *the Labdakids / whose life is suffering and pain* Eteokles and Polyneikes are Labdakids as descendants of Labdakos, father of Laios; the patronymic puts their strife into the context of the curse upon the whole royal house. They also share the epithet of Ares himself in the opening line of the ode, *polymokhthos*, "of the many toils."

928 *with gold pins* These are presumably the same as the "spikes of iron" stuck through Oedipus' ankles at line 19, though the apparent inconsistency

of the materials has led some to take up the suggestion of the scholiast that the reference is to the golden clasps with which Oedipus blinded himself (56).

967-1153 Third episode

984f. war . . . *against Eumolpos* Euripides, with fine irony, connects Teiresias' "saving" of Thebes in this scene with a similar incident at Athens. His victory there consisted of announcing to King Erectheus the necessity of sacrificing his daughter in order to win a war he was waging against the Eleusinians led by Eumolpos. This was the subject of Euripides' *Erectheus*, produced a decade or more before the *Phoenician Women*. A long fragment survives in which Queen Praxithea consents to the sacrifice in order to save her land.

1154-1209 Third stasimon

1155f. *wingèd child of earth, / of Ekhidna* This is the Sphinx, child of an earth-spirit and consequently regarded as earth-born herself.

1180f. *Apollo's priestess sent / pitiful Oedipus* The Pythia at Delphi merely told Oedipus that he would murder his father and marry his mother; he went to Thebes on his flight from those he imagined to be his parents in Korinth.

1210-1416 Fourth episode

1217 *warding off every attack* This is followed in the manuscripts by a line that is quite otiose and said by the scholiast to be missing from many copies: "What new word do you come to announce to me?"

1245ff. *Then / Parthenopaios* The elaborate description of the seven Argive commanders, which goes through line 1277, has been suspected as an interpolated substitute for the Antigone/tutor scene (lines 84-233). Aside from its duplication of the matter of those lines, the objections to this passage involve a certain number of stylistic and linguistic oddities conveniently reported and discussed by D. J. Mastronarde, *Phoenix* 32 (1978), 105-28.

1255ff. *The sign / was Argos* These lines are apparently corrupt, but no entirely satisfactory emendation or interpretation has been proposed. We take the text to suggest a picture of Argos, with some eyes open and some closed, against a starry field. Argos' eyes are likened to constellations that keep emerging and disappearing as time passes: at any moment some are to be seen.

1265 *the fillies of Potniai* An equivocal emblem: These mares belonged to a son of Sisyphos named Glaukos, who prevented them from mating. In revenge, Aphrodite, goddess of love, turned them against him, and they ate their master alive.

1275f. *a hundred hydra heads, / the glory of the Argives* Adrastos' shield has a depiction of the Lernaean hydra, which Herakles slew, and whose venom made his arrows deadly.

1362f. *silence in / the armies* There follows in the manuscripts a redundant line apparently interpolated by someone who felt that Eteokles' speech needed a clearer marker, and reported by the scholiast to be missing in most copies: "He spoke, 'O leaders of the land of Hellas. . . .' "

1369 *this land is all his* Three lines follow in the manuscripts: "You, o Argives, cast aside the fight and go to your country, not leaving your lives here. And the people of the sown-men suffice, who lie dead." The last line is a metrical and linguistic makeshift. The first two are unobjectionable as Greek, but pallid and anti-climactic.

1393 *There's terrible danger* This is followed in the manuscripts by two lines: "And the prize is fearful; there will be tears for you, deprived of two children on one day." This bland anticipation of the double death is seemingly confected out of two lines from Sophocles' *Antigone*.

1415 *my life is saved* The manuscripts add: "If you come after, we're lost, and you die." This is the same as line 1114, and appears to be an interpolation here.

1417-51 Fourth *stasimon*

1452 1907 *Exodos* This term, defined by Aristotle as the remainder of the tragedy following the final choral ode, obviously includes more than the characters' departure from the stage, or what we would call the final scene. The exodos of the *Phoenician Women* is unusually long and rich.

1636f. *you lived up / to your quarrelsome name*   The name *Polyneikes* can be derived from the Greek words *polus*, "much," and *neikos*, "strife."

1735f. *crimson libation / of cold blood*   There is a grim play on the custom of offering libations (of wine, not blood) in honor of the dead.

1799f. *crowning / this corpse*   This is not a special tribute, but simply a customary part of Greek funerary practice.

1801 *death for his pains*   The manuscripts add a line borrowed almost without change from Sophocles, *Antigone* 29: "Leave him unwept, without a tomb, a feast for birds."

1841 *the daughters of Danaos*   Forty-nine of the fifty daughters killed their husbands, the sons of Danaos' brother Aigyptos, on their wedding night.

1873 *Holy Kolonos, home of the horse god*   Poseidon, god of horses as well as of the sea, had a sanctuary at this suburb of Athens. This line, assuming that it is authentic, is the first mention of Oedipus' death on Attic soil, a story enacted a few years later in Sophocles' last play, *Oedipus at Colonus*.

1901 *and death somewhere*   As indicated in the Introduction, the authenticity of much of the final scenes, from the entrance of Oedipus, has been suspected. While we have chosen to retain most of the received text, we find it impossible to credit to Euripides the bizarre exchange which now follows:

ANTIGONE: Leaving tears of yearning with my maiden-friends, I go far away from the land of my fathers, wandering in no maidenly way. OEDIPUS: Ah, the excellence of your spirit! ANTIGONE: In my father's misfortunes at least it will bring me glory. Wretched me, for the outrages against you and my brother, who is gone from our house, an unburied corpse, miserable, whom I shall cover with earth in secret, even if I must die for it, my father. OEDIPUS: Appear before your companions. ANTIGONE: Enough of my lamentations. OEDIPUS: But prayers before the altars . . . ANTIGONE: They are sated with my woes. OEDIPUS: Go at least where is the precinct of Bromios, not to be trodden, on the mountain of the Maenads . . . ANTIGONE: To him for whom I once ran on the mountains, dressed in the Kadmean fawn-skin, in Semele's holy rout? To render thankless service to the gods?

To go no further, Antigone and Oedipus have already started into exile (cf. 1874ff.), and there is no apparent motivation for the visits Oedipus suggests. This appears to be the work of a bungler.

1902ff. *O people of a famous land*   We include these lines in order to give some semblance of a closing, but without any confidence that they are the lines Euripides wrote to end his play. They are closely modeled on the closing lines of Sophocles' *Oedipus Tyrannus*; the people addressed in 1902 cannot be the Chorus, but no one else is present. After 1902 we omit a line almost identical to Sophocles, *Oedipus Tyrannus* 1525, but with the wrong verbal person for this context: "he who knew the glorious riddles and was a very great man." We have also excised the closing choral tag, shared with Euripides' *Orestes* and *Iphigeneia in Tauris*, but singularly out of place at the end of this play: "O great awesome victory, keep hold of my life, and do not stop crowning me."

GLOSSARY

ACHERON, river of Hades.

ADRASTOS, king of Argos and father-in-law of Polyneikes.

AGENOR, king of Tyre, father of Europa and Kadmos.

AITOLIA, region of Greece north of the Gulf of Korinth, between Phokis to the east and Acarnania to the west.

AMPHIARAOS, priest and seer, Argive commander in the war against Thebes.

AMPHION, Theban hero, whose lyre-playing caused the city walls to rise. Said by Euripides to be a son of Zeus and divine, along with his brother Zethos.

AMYMONE, daughter of Danaos, loved by Poseidon.

ANTIGONE, daughter of Oedipus and Jokasta.

APOLLO, god of prophecy whose oracle at Delphi, source of the prophecies concerning the house of Laios, is the final destination of the Phoenician women.

ARES, god of war.

ARGOS, 1. a being of human form, covered with eyes over his whole body, who guarded Io after she had been changed into a heifer; 2. a city in the Peloponnese, where Polyneikes married and lived while in exile, and whose army he leads against Thebes.

ARTEMIS, a goddess associated with wild animals and the hunt, daughter of Leto and twin sister of Apollo.

ATALANTA, a huntress of Arcadia, who bore Parthenopaios to Meleager.

ATTICA, a region of Greece surrounding Athens.

BROMIOS, cult name of Dionysos, "the Rumbler."

DANAANS, a name used of the Argives because of their descent from Danaos.

DANAOS, descendant of Io, father of fifty daughters, all but one of whom murdered their bridegrooms.

DELPHI, a town in central Greece, site of the famous sanctuary and oracle of Apollo.

DEMETER, goddess of grain and mother of Persephone.

DIONYSOS, god of wine and ecstatic possession, born at Thebes from Semele, whom Zeus fertilized and destroyed by a bolt of lightning.

DIRKE, a river at Thebes.

DODONA, site of an ancient and famous oracle of Zeus in the mountains of western Greece.

EKHIDNA, an earth daimon, used by Euripides to symbolize the awesome power of the earth itself, which gives birth to the Sphinx.

EPAPHOS, divine son of Zeus and Io, ancestor of both Thebans and Phoenicians through Agenor, king of Tyre.

ERINYES, or Furies, ancient goddesses who embody the curse within a bloodline.

ETEOKLES, son of Oedipus in power at Thebes.

EUMOLPOS, king of the Eleusinians, slain in battle by King Erectheus of Athens.

GORGON, monster in woman's form with writhing snakes for hair and a face so hideous that all who saw it turned to stone.

HADES, divine ruler of the kingdom of the dead below ground.

HAIMON, son of Kreon, engaged to Antigone.

HARMONIA, daughter of Ares and Aphrodite, wife of Kadmos.

HEKATE, a chthonian goddess often closely associated or identified with Artemis.

HERA, wife of Zeus and queen of the Olympian gods.

HIPPOMEDON, Argive commander.

IO, an Argive princess loved by Zeus, who turned her into a heifer and pursued her to Egypt, where she bore Epaphos and became ancestor, after many generations, to Thebans and Phoenicians alike.

ISMENE, daughter of Oedipus and Jokasta.

ISMENOS, a river of Thebes.

IXION, a mortal who attempted to seduce the goddess Hera and was eternally punished by being attached to a revolving wheel in Tartaros.

JOKASTA, queen of Thebes, sister of Kreon, widow of Laios, mother and wife of Oedipus.

KADMOS, founder of Thebes, son of King Agenor of Tyre.

KAPANEUS, Argive commander.

KASTALIA, spring in Mount Parnassos at Delphi.

KITHAIRON, mountain to the south of Thebes.

KOLONOS, a small settlement just north of Athens where Oedipus found refuge and was buried.

KREON, brother of Jokasta, father of Haimon and Menoikeus.

KYPRIS, cult name of Aphrodite, goddess of love.

LABDAKOS, father of Laios; his descendants are often referred to as Labakids.

LAIOS, son of Labdakos, father of Oedipus, who killed him.

LERNA, a coastal marsh south of Argos.

LETO, goddess of the Titan generation, mother of Apollo and Artemis.

LOXIAS, cult name of Apollo.

MAINALOS, mountain in Arcadia, home of Atalanta.

MENOIKEUS, 1. father of Kreon; 2. son of Kreon.

MYCENAE, city dominating the northeast corner of the Argive plain.

NEMESIS, goddess of retribution.

NIOBE, wife of Amphion, boasted of her many children (six or seven daughters in most accounts and an equal number of sons), saying that Leto had only two. Apollo and Artemis, angered by the insult to their mother, killed all of Niobe's children.

OEDIPUS, son of Laios and Jokasta; killed Laios, married Jokasta. Father of Eteokles, Polyneikes, Antigone, Ismene.

PARTHENOPAIOS, an Arcadian, son of Atalanta, and a commander of the Argive army.

PERIKLYMENOS, defender of Thebes who slays Parthenopaios in battle.

PERSEPHONE, daughter of Demeter, carried to the underworld by Hades and kept there as his queen for part of each year.

PHOIBOS, cult name of Apollo.

PHOKIS, region of Greece which included Delphi and Mount Parnassos.

POLYBOS, King of Korinth, foster-father of Oedipus.

POLYDOROS, son of Kadmos and Harmonia, father of Labdakos.

POLYNEIKES, son of Oedipus, exiled by his brother Eteokles.

POSEIDON, Olympian god associated with the sea and other waters, and with horses.

POTNIAI, a village just south of Thebes where there was a well said to madden horses that drank at it.

PROMETHEUS, god of the Titan generation who brought fire to mankind.

SELANAIA, the moon, identified with the goddess Artemis.

SPHINX, a monster with the head of a woman, the wings of a bird, and the hindquarters of a lion. She killed those who attempted to answer her riddle, until Oedipus succeeded and destroyed her.

TARTAROS, the lowest reaches of the underworld.

TEIRESIAS, blind Theban prophet.

TEUMESSOS, hill outside Thebes from which the Argives attack the city gates.

THESPROTIA, a part of the mountainous region of Epiros in western Greece, here mentioned as the home of Zeus's shrine at Dodona.

THESSALY, a region of northern Greece.

TYDEUS, son of Oineus, exiled for bloodshed from his native Kalydon, marries a daughter of Adrastos and joins Polyneikes' expedition against Thebes.

ZEPHYROS, god of the West Wind.

ZETHOS, brother of Amphion. According to Euripides, the brothers are sons of Zeus and received divine honors in Thebes.

ZEUS, ruler of the Olympian gods.